Access Your Online Resources

101 Activities to Help Children Get on Together contains a number of printable online materials, designed to ensure this resource best supports your professional needs.

Go to https://resourcecentre.routledge.com/speechmark and click on the cover of this book.

Answer the question prompt using your copy of the book to gain access to the online content.

'Jenny Mosley is quite simply a legend, whose work has inspired countless teachers and support staff to create the kinds of classrooms and playgrounds in which children can truly thrive. Her bestselling series of *Games* books, written with the equally brilliant Helen Sonnet, has only become more relevant in recent years, as schools across the UK grapple with the many challenges facing children today.'

Jean Gross CBE, *bestselling author and former government Communication Champion for children*

'Just what we needed. We loved the other three but this one is very "hands on" and encourages teamwork and children to work with others they wouldn't usually choose to – but because they love the activities they just get on!'

Emma Wayper, *Deputy Head, Watercliffe Meadow Primary School, Sheffield*

'An incredibly useful resource, especially at a time when more children than ever need emotional support. This book is easy to navigate, brilliantly introduced, and packed with practical, impactful activities. Jenny Mosley's expertise shines through in this comprehensive collection. It's an invaluable tool for anyone working with children.'

Sarah Watkins, *lecturer, author and early years specialist*

101 Activities to Help Children Get on Together

101 Activities to Help Children Get on Together is full of motivating and engaging activities that will teach children the essential skills of co-operation. Drawing on the authors' extensive experience, the activities are enjoyable, appealing and purposeful.

The book employs both physical and creative activities to encourage and develop teamwork. Each activity is just a starting point, inspiring readers to adapt it to their own classes and topics taught, with variations also suggested. The activities will enable you to assess a child's ability to co-operate, target specific ways to develop their skills and promote positive experiences through working with others.

Designed for busy practitioners and educators, this revised edition with resources available to download, will help you to encourage stronger co-operation in your classes, contributing to better relationships and more effective learning.

Jenny Mosley is the founder of Jenny Mosley Training Consultancies and originator of the highly acclaimed 'Quality Circle Time Model' that is used in thousands of early years settings, primary and secondary schools, nationally and internationally. Her unique approach has featured on BBC Television's Teaching Today, Channel 4 and Open University programmes, in addition to the national press and numerous education journals.

Helen Sonnet is a teacher and author with over 30 years of experience working with children with special needs.

101 Games and Activities
Jenny Mosley and Helen Sonnet

101 Games for Better Behaviour
Supporting Feelings and Building Emotional Understanding
ISBN: 9781041083894 (pbk)

101 Games for Self-Esteem
Building Confidence and Motivation
ISBN: 9781041083863 (pbk)

101 Games for Social Skills
Exploring Positive Relationships and Healthy Interactions
ISBN: 9781041084044 (pbk)

101 Activities to Help Children Get on Together
Building Co-operation and Belonging
ISBN: 9781041084068 (pbk)

101 Activities to Help Children Get on Together

Building Co-operation and Belonging

Revised Edition

Jenny Mosley and Helen Sonnet

LONDON AND NEW YORK

Designed cover image: Getty Images

Revised edition published 2026
by Routledge
4 Park Square, Milton Park, Abingdon, Oxon, OX14 4RN

and by Routledge
605 Third Avenue, New York, NY 10158

Routledge is an imprint of the Taylor & Francis Group, an informa business

© 2026 Jenny Mosley and Helen Sonnet

The right of Jenny Mosley and Helen Sonnet to be identified as authors of this work has been asserted in accordance with sections 77 and 78 of the Copyright, Designs and Patents Act 1988.

Illustrations © Mark Cripps

All rights reserved. The purchase of this copyright material confers the right on the purchasing institution to photocopy or download pages which bear the support material icon and a copyright line at the bottom of the page. No other parts of this book may be reprinted or reproduced or utilised in any form or by any electronic, mechanical, or other means, now known or hereafter invented, including photocopying and recording, or in any information storage or retrieval system, without permission in writing from the publishers.

Trademark notice: Product or corporate names may be trademarks or registered trademarks, and are used only for identification and explanation without intent to infringe.

First edition originally published by LDA 2008

British Library Cataloguing-in-Publication Data
A catalogue record for this book is available from the British Library

ISBN: 978-1-041-08410-5 (hbk)
ISBN: 978-1-041-08406-8 (pbk)
ISBN: 978-1-003-64525-2 (ebk)

DOI: 10.4324/9781003645252

Typeset in Interstate
by Deanta Global Publishing Services, Chennai, India

Access the online resources: https://resourcecentre.routledge.com/speechmark

Contents

Acknowledgements	*xii*
Foreword	*xiii*
Introduction	*xiv*

1 Working in a Pair — 1

Sort and share	*2*
Behind the door	*3*
Facing the facts	*4*
Where's the bear?	*5*
What's in the box?	*6*
Change your partner, please	*7*
Capturing counters	*8*
Co-operation under pressure	*9*
Bag the blocks	*10*
Measuring up	*11*
Further activities	*12*

2 Playing Detectives — 13

Crimestoppers	*14*
Eagle eyes	*15*
Superspy	*16*
Who is the mystery person?	*17*
Secret signs	*18*
Pick up the pieces	*19*
Building up a picture	*20*

Bearnapped!	*21*
Finders keepers	*22*
Sneezy subjects	*23*
Further activities	*24*

3 Expending Energy Together — 25

Treasure trove	*26*
Get weaving	*27*
Heads or tails?	*28*
Group tug of war	*29*
Steppingstones	*30*
Pass the ball, please	*31*
Catch a snake	*32*
Chariot racing	*33*
The hungry bear	*34*
Beanbags and blindfolds	*35*
Further activities	*36*

4 Investigations — 37

Float or sink?	*38*
The balancing man	*39*
Balloon blowing	*40*
Taste trials	*41*
Strong strips	*42*
Metamorphosis	*43*
A warm bed	*44*
Working on eggshells	*45*
Telephone trials	*46*
Building bridges	*47*
Further activities	*48*

5 Letters and Words — 49

Word race — *50*
Paper chains — *51*
Song sorting — *52*
Word circle — *53*
Initial success — *54*
Print sprint — *55*
Picture perfect — *56*
Question collection — *57*
What's your favourite…? — *58*
Car capers — *59*
Further activities — *60*

6 Art Projects — 61

Hands-on printing — *62*
Quick-sketch artist — *63*
Garden designs — *64*
Collective collage — *65*
Artistic recollections — *66*
Landscape gardening — *67*
The running man — *68*
Guess who? — *69*
Shaping up — *70*
Striking squares — *71*
Further activities — *72*

7 Drama Projects — 73

Stop motion — *74*
Four characters — *75*
Rescue team — *76*
Masterful mimes — *77*

Around the campfire	78
Where did that come from?	79
Well-versed tableaux	80
Idiom antics	81
Perfectly formed	83
Elf wishes	84
Further activities	85

8 Activities for Outdoors   86

Box the balls	87
Add or subtract?	88
Armchair hockey	89
Colourful steps	91
Crossing countries	92
A spoonful of water	93
Passing palette	94
Cuckoo	95
Charitable actions	96
Animal magic	97
Playground projects	98
Further activities	99

9 Rhythm and Dance   100

Clap happy	101
Taking steps	102
Stepping out	103
We're the best	104
Standing ovation	105
Symbolic sequences	106
Talking drums	107
Back and forth	108
It's all in the name	109

Contents xi

Fruit juice	*110*
Further activities	*111*

10 Construction — 112

Brilliant board games	*113*
Inspired instruments	*114*
Are you receiving me?	*115*
Architectural adventures	*116*
Stage setting	*117*
Spy wear	*118*
Create a castle	*119*
Sculpture gardens	*120*
Water works	*121*
Hideaway	*122*
Further activities	*123*

Printable Materials — 125

Behind the door (1)	*126*
Behind the door (2)	*127*
Facing the facts	*128*
Where's the bear?	*129*
Pick up the pieces	*130*
Building up a picture	*131*
The balancing man	*132*
Car capers	*133*
The running man	*134*
Four characters	*135*
We're the best	*136*
Spy wear	*137*
Sculpture gardens	*138*

Training and Resources — 139

Acknowledgements

We would love to thank Alison Foyle and Jane Madeley for judging that the time was right for the republication of all four *101* books. They have given us a lot of support, encouragement and warmth along the way. Molly Kavanagh is a great editorial assistant and was always there to help us with the tricky technical bits.

We are so glad that, post-pandemic, there has been such a surge of interest in the importance of play. Interestingly, there is now agreement that adults need to play as well. We have always encouraged all our group facilitators and teachers to join in with the group members, as it makes it more enjoyable.

The National Institute of Play states that 'playful adults are more likely to employ positive coping mechanisms such as acceptance and reframing in stressful situations' (Proyer, 2012). So, dear reader, have fun with everyone!

Jenny Mosley and Helen Sonnet

References

Proyer, RT (2012) 'Examining playfulness in adults: Testing its correlation with personality, positive psychological functioning, goal aspirations, and multi-methodically assessed ingenuity.' *Psychological Test and Assessment Modeling*, 54(2), 103-127.

Foreword

Jenny Mosley is quite simply a legend, whose work has inspired countless teachers and support staff to create the kinds of classrooms and playgrounds in which children can truly thrive. Her bestselling series of *Games* books, written with the equally brilliant Helen Sonnet, has only become more relevant in recent years, as schools across the UK grapple with the many challenges facing children today.

Games promote a sense of belonging in a class or group. And belonging (or lack thereof) is emerging as a key issue affecting children's learning, behaviour and attendance. When we experience feelings of belonging to a group, our body produces a cocktail of hormones that makes us feel calm and able to focus. Conversely, if we are unsure whether we belong we are anxious, constantly monitoring the environment for cues as to whether or how we can fit in. Creating a cohesive class, where there is a sense of group identity, avoids this and frees up children to concentrate on learning.

The games in this book also build essential social and emotional skills, such as self-awareness, self-regulation, empathy and the social skills of co-operation and conflict resolution. Research shows us that teaching these skills can make a significant contribution to achievement, as well as to a range of other important outcomes, from mental health to employability.

Flexible in their use – from playground to start and end of day, PE warm-ups or circle time – the game ideas that Jenny and Helen share here should play a part in every child's day. Some people might argue that this is a waste of learning time. The evidence, however, suggests otherwise. I cannot recommend these books highly enough.

Jean Gross *CBE*
Bestselling author and former government
Communication Champion for children

Introduction

Welcome to a book of motivating and purposeful activities written to teach the children you work with the essential skills of co-operation! There are activities provided that will help in many different ways, and you are sure to find many to suit your children's needs. Some of the activities are designed to develop a sense of belonging and team spirit, while others will help children to work in partnership and enhance their sensitivity towards their peers – who may think and express themselves differently.

Unlike the other three *101* books, which are 'in the moment' games-based, some of the activities outlined here require the adult to get the game ready prior to starting. You may need time to photocopy or print, to collect together sufficient resources or to prepare the equipment. Each activity is clearly labelled with any equipment sourced at the beginning – it's therefore a good idea to check the list over to ensure you have time to prepare. This might take a few minutes but the activities are worth it!

The activities in this book are not designed to be solely an enjoyable way to spend time together. If used appropriately, they can be a powerful and influential means to motivate and inspire. With this in mind, always remember that it is a good idea to set aside a little time at the end of an activity to discuss which skills were focused on. Children learn best through hands-on experience but giving them time to organise and express their thoughts and feelings deepens their understanding and makes the purpose of an activity even more beneficial. You will probably need to prompt the children by asking questions initially but they will soon realise what you want them to look out for, and then all they will need is the time to formulate questions and listen to the opinions of others. By this, you will be encouraging another level of co-operation – attentive speaking and listening.

As you watch children engage in these activities, you will be able to assess their strengths and weaknesses. Which children are able to co-operate with ease? Who needs to learn to mitigate their need to control? Who would benefit from help to overcome shyness and lack of social confidence? Because the activities encourage co-operation, you will be able to see who needs help and who can be cited as a good role model.

The activities in this book focus on different aspects of co-operation. Some activities are energetic and require space, while others are quieter and more reflective. Each activity has a clear purpose, a list of resources along with detailed instructions, as well as general comments and advice. Sometimes suggestions are included to help you to deepen the impact of an activity. Don't be afraid to adapt activities to suit your setting or change themes to fit with specific curriculum areas. Use the ideas flexibly, adding your own personal touches.

The most exciting and effective activities are those that children make their own. We are sure that you will find ones like that here – activities that children will want to play repeatedly and teach to younger children in your setting. The opportunities provided by well-designed activities are numerous. You will doubtless discover that your children will make up their own variations that they will enjoy playing independently at playtime and at home.

1 Working in a Pair

Working with a partner is particularly valuable for children who are quiet or withdrawn, who might find participation in a larger group daunting – especially if other members are confident and assertive. Shyer children might find it difficult to make their voice heard or might prefer to remain quiet and let others air their views. In a paired activity, these children have their turn to contribute clearly defined for them. They do not have to vie for an opportunity to take part or face the unwelcome prospect of being on display before a larger audience.

A paired activity may be used as a lesson starter to focus the children's attention and encourage co-operative practice. It may also be used as a calming strategy following a session of group or whole-class activities.

Sort and share

This activity works well as a standalone game and as a way to sort children into pairs.

Resources

None.

What to do

Ask the children to line up in order of height. Divide them into pairs starting at one end of the line. Ask each pair to choose which child will start. This child tells their partner their ideal holiday destination. They then swap roles and repeat the exercise. Ask each pair in turn to tell the rest of the children what destination their partner chose.

Repeat the activity, asking the children to sort themselves by a different criterion – for example, alphabetical order by first name or the number of their front door at home. Vary the subject of the information to be shared.

Comments

You could try sorting the children by opinions as well as just factual information – for example, what they think about climate change, the royal family or screen time for children. You can order them based on where their answer falls in a spectrum from good to bad or yes to no. They can then discuss their opinions in pairs. You could make this more interesting by pairing up children from different ends of the spectrum and seeing whether they change their minds after discussing the issue with their partner.

Behind the door

This activity is an enjoyable way to stimulate creative thinking.

Resources

Enough enlarged photocopies or printouts of page 126 or 127, pencils, paper and scissors for each pair.

What to do

Put the children into mixed-ability pairs. Give each pair the resources they need. Ask them to think of items that might be found behind the door or gate shown on their photocopy or printout downloaded from the online resources. For example, there might be a sword, a knight, a princess, a goblet, a four-poster bed or a crown behind the door of a castle. Alternatively, there might be a flower, a wheelbarrow, a ladybird, a swing, a plant pot or a garden chair behind a garden gate.

The children draw or write their items on their piece of paper and cut them out. When the children have completed this task, join the pairs together to form groups of four. Pairs must not show each other the items that they have prepared. Each pair takes it in turn to put one of their items behind their photocopied door or gate. They then challenge the other pair in their group to work out what it is by asking questions. Play several rounds of the game.

Comments

Discuss the types of questions that the children might ask before they begin the second part of the activity – for example, 'Is it alive?', 'Is it man-made?', 'Can you eat it?', 'What colour is it?', 'What is it made from?', 'How big is it?' Tell the children to work quietly in the guessing phase so as not to give away what the items are to other groups of four in case you want to play further rounds in different groups.

Facing the facts

This is a great game for boosting self-esteem.

Resources

A photocopy or printout of page 128 for each child. Coloured pencils, scissors and a spotted 1-6 dice for each pair.

What to do

Put the children into pairs and give each child a photocopy or printout of page 128 to colour in. Once completed, have them cut out the items shown. The children then take turns in their pairs to roll their dice. For each number rolled, they collect the following item(s) and complete the related sentence:

- 1: Face ('I like my [chosen part of the body]').
- 2: Both eyes ('I like to look at …').
- 3: Nose ('I like to smell … ').
- 4: Both ears ('I like to listen to … ').
- 5: Mouth ('I like to eat … ').
- 6: Crown ('I am good at … ').

If they already have the item(s) for the number rolled, they skip that go. The winner is the first child in each pair to fully assemble their photocopied face.

Comments

Before you begin, ask the children to remember one of the sentences that their partner says during the game. When most/all of the faces are complete, call the children into a circle and ask each child in turn to tell the group their partner's sentence.

Where's the bear?

This enjoyable activity will encourage creativity.

Resources

A photocopy or printout of page 129, coloured pencils and coloured stickers for each pair.

What to do

Put the children into pairs and give each pair a different number. Hand out the resources listed above. Discuss the types of stalls that might be found at a market – flower, fruit, toy, clothing, toiletries, hardware and so on. Give the children time to draw different items from each of the stalls on their photocopy or printout downloaded from the online resources. They may colour in their drawings.

After sufficient time, ask the children to imagine that a small child has lost their teddy bear at the market. Each pair must decide on the stall at which the child left their bear and draw a faint mark on the back of their photocopy or printout behind their chosen stall. The pairs then move around the room, guessing where the bear can be found on the photocopies or printouts of the other pairs and collecting guesses from pairs on their own sheet. A pair makes a guess by placing a sticker on their chosen stall on each photocopy or printout. They must write the number of their pair on the sticker. Once all the pairs have done this, they can take turns to announce which pair(s) guessed correctly on their photocopies or printouts.

Comments

It would be helpful if each pair placed their photocopy or printout on a hard surface before asking the others to decide where to place their stickers, to prevent the paper from creasing or getting damaged.

What's in the box?

This enjoyable activity promotes active listening, creative thinking and the sharing of ideas.

Resources

Several matching containers with lids. Partially fill each container with a different substance – such as split peas, rice, gravel, buttons or oat flakes – before sealing it firmly. Number each container. You will also need a sheet of paper and pencil per pair.

What to do

Put the children into pairs. Ask a child to shake the first container. Each pair listens to the sound made and then makes a note of what they think is in the container. Repeat this process for the other containers. Call the children back together to discuss their answers. Open each container in turn to reveal what's inside.

Comments

If you think the children could find this activity difficult, display a list of the contents of the containers as a prompt or reduce the number of containers.

Change your partner, please

The children will enjoy the anticipation involved in this game.

Resources

None. You need plenty of space to move around in.

What to do

Put the children into pairs, apart from one child. Give the children instructions to carry out with their partners – for example:

- Stand face to face.
- Stand back to back.
- Touch right hand to right hand.
- Shake hands.
- Perform a high five.

Explain that if you call, 'Change your partner, please,' each child must find a new partner as quickly as possible. At the same time, the child who is without a partner must try to find one too. The child who is left on their own after the changeover must try to find a partner next time.

Comments

Vary the speed at which you give the instructions, depending on how fast you want the game to be.

Capturing counters

This is a simple and enjoyable game to play in pairs.

Resources

Sufficient plastic counters to hand out up to 20 per child, depending on age/ability.

What to do

Ask the children to form pairs. Give each child up to 20 counters, depending on age/ability. Ensure that each child in a pair has an equal number. Each child puts their counters in their right hand. One child then transfers some of their counters to their left hand without their partner seeing. Their partner must try to guess how many counters are now in their left hand. If they guess correctly, they get to keep the counters. The roles are reversed for the next round. At the end of the game, the winner is the child in each pair with the most counters.

Comments

You might like to stage a competition to find the champion counter capturer.

Co-operation under pressure

This is a useful activity for promoting co-operation in pairs.

Resources

Two blindfolds and a large cuddly toy.

What to do

Put the children into pairs. Ask them to form a large circle, with each child standing next to their partner. Choose a pair to wear the blindfolds. Place the cuddly toy somewhere inside the circle. On your command, the pair wearing the blindfolds must work together to try to find the toy. They may decide to hold hands and search the area together or work individually, calling out to each other as they search. Once they have found the toy or an agreed amount of time has elapsed, they return to their places in the circle, another pair is chosen and the toy is moved to a different position.

Comments

You could use a sand timer to make the activity more exciting. After a few rounds, discuss which search methods are proving to be the most effective.

To add a competitive element, you might wish to time each pair to see who is quickest to find the toy. If the pairs find it easy to locate the toy, use a smaller object.

Bag the blocks

This game helps children to develop strategies for a successful partnership.

Resources

A large number of Multilink cubes or similar small blocks and three bags.

What to do

Put the children into pairs and ask them to form a circle, with each child standing next to their partner. Number the pairs around the circle from one to five. (This number is based on a group of 30 children; reduce the number range if your group is smaller.)

Place the Multilink cubes in the centre of the circle, along with the bags. Call out a number from your range. Each pair with that number holds hands and runs round the outside of the circle in a clockwise direction. When they get back to their starting point, they enter the circle, while continuing to hold hands. One child in each pair picks up a bag with their free hand and holds it open, while their partner picks up a cube and places it in the bag. Players should pick up only one cube at a time. As soon as you have called out your number, the remaining children in the circle begin a countdown from a specified number which allows enough time for the running around and some frantic collecting. Once the countdown has ended, each pair inside the circle must stop collecting and count how many cubes they have in their bag. The cubes are then returned to the centre of the circle along with the bags and a new round begins.

Comments

Make this game more difficult by getting the children to wear large gloves, such as gardening or oven gloves, on their spare hands.

Measuring up

This is a useful activity to encourage paired discussion.

Resources

A slip of paper and a pencil for each pair.

What to do

Put the children into pairs and give each a different measuring task, such as measuring the length/width/height of:

- The room in full strides.
- The room in heel-to-toe steps.
- A bookcase in hand spans.
- The door in index-finger lengths.
- The cupboard in forearm lengths.
- The hall in arm spans.

Ask each pair to write their task and the measurement taken on a slip of paper. Call the children together and allow each pair in turn to state their task. Ask the other children to suggest what the measurement might be in each case. The pair with the closest guess gets a point.

Comments

Before the measuring task begins, ensure that the children understand what you mean by the different units of measurement.

Further activities

Treasure hunt

Play this game outside where there is more space. It is designed for six pairs at a time. Give each pair a piece of 'treasure'. One child in each pair puts on a blindfold, while their partner hides the treasure some distance away and moves away from it. They then shout instructions to their partner, telling them where to go to find the treasure. As there are six children shouting instructions at the same time, the blindfolded children must try to concentrate on their partner's voice in order to find their treasure. The first pair to succeed is the winner.

You can't say that

Create a collection of cards, each with a different letter of the alphabet on it, omitting Q, V, X, Y and Z. Produce another set of cards, each with a different category on it, such as pets, fruit, sports, vegetables and colours. Place each card set in a different container. Ask a pair of children to take one card from each container. They then take it in turns to say an item in the given category that does not have the nominated letter in it. They are not allowed to repeat an item or hesitate. If they do, they sit down with their partner after having chosen two cards for the next pair.

Rock, paper, scissors II

Put the children into pairs and ask each pair to devise a different version of 'Rock, paper, scissors'. Share ideas and choose a couple of the most popular versions to start a new playground craze.

2 Playing Detectives

Children will enjoy playing at being detectives in the following activities, interpreting clues and unravelling mysteries. The activities encourage creative thinking and the pooling of ideas to reach a conclusion. They are an excellent way to get children talking together, discussing their views and developing logical strategies to solve problems.

Crimestoppers

This activity enables children to practise observational and recording skills.

Resources

Props for your crime scene; paper and pencils for each group.

What to do

Before the children arrive, set up the room as a crime scene. Basil Bunny has climbed in through an open window and stolen the contents of a biscuit jar. You might set up the following clues:

- Some cotton wool by an open window, representing fluff from the rabbit's tail.
- A handkerchief bearing the initials BB.
- A rabbit's paw print on the floor.
- A discarded half-eaten carrot.
- Some biscuit crumbs.
- An overturned empty biscuit jar.

Divide the children into mixed-ability groups of four or five. Ask each group to make a sketch of the crime scene, numbering any clues they find. Ask the children to talk quietly in their groups to work out what has happened. After an appropriate amount of time, call the groups together to share their findings, including what they think each clue might indicate.

Comments

If possible, space out each group during the discussion phase of the activity, so that they cannot overhear each other. Ask the children which clues they thought were the most important and why.

The groups could each devise a crime scene with clues to use on another occasion. They could use nursery rhymes – such as 'The Queen of Hearts' or 'Little Bo Peep' – as a starting point.

Eagle eyes

This is a good activity to encourage children to pool their ideas.

Resources

Someone who is unknown to the children; paper and pencils for each group.

What to do

Arrange for someone whom the children don't know to visit your room at some point. Have them enter, look around, walk to the back of the room and remove an object that you have agreed with them beforehand. They can say one sentence – perhaps in an assumed accent – such as, 'Just borrowing this – don't let me interrupt!'

The next day, tell the children that you can't remember who came in to borrow something yesterday. Ask them for their help. Divide them into small groups and ask them to write down all the details they can remember about the stranger: sex, age, height, hair and eye colour, clothing and any other details. After an appropriate amount of time, call the groups together to compare their findings. Then, if possible, ask the stranger to come in dressed in the same way as previously, so that the children can check the accuracy of their notes.

Comments

Ask your helper to enhance their appearance with various accessories, such as a hat, a bag, a pair of glasses, a pair of gloves, a buttonhole and so on.

Superspy

This game requires children to work together to achieve specific goals.

Resources

A book. You need plenty of space to move around in.

What to do

Place the book in an obvious location in the room. Refer to it as a book of secret information of vital importance. Choose two children to leave the room and have them decide between themselves which of them will be the spy and which the accomplice. At the same time, ask the other children to stand in a space in the room. Choose a child in the room to be the guard.

Call the two children back into the room. They must work together to try to steal the book. The spy must try to grab it and escape from the room without being apprehended by the guard. The accomplice must try to confuse the guard – for example, by making sudden lunges for the book and then pulling back; blocking the spy from the guard's line of sight; or pointing or shouting to distract them. The guard cannot make a move until the spy has picked up the book. If they manage to touch the spy, the game is over. If the spy escapes, congratulate them and return the book. Repeat the game with different children.

Comments

Prior to the game, discuss the different techniques that the spy and their accomplice might use to confuse the guard. Warn the children not to watch the guard too closely, as this might give away their identity. You may want to agree on a starting position for the guard, to ensure that they don't stand right next to the book.

Who is the mystery person?

This intriguing activity will promote creative thinking.

Resources

Small items from a person's handbag or coat pocket that reveal details about the owner (eg, sex, age, job); paper and pencils for each group.

What to do

Divide the children into groups of four or five. Explain that a person suffering from amnesia had a number of items in their coat pocket/handbag. Show them the items. Ask the children to discuss them in their groups and try to build up a profile of the person. The items might include:

- A train ticket.
- A letter written on headed business paper.
- A list of football fixtures.
- A family photograph.
- A reminder to attend an eye test.
- An invitation to attend a 40th birthday party.
- A library card from the municipal library.

After an appropriate amount of time, call the groups together to compare their findings.

Comments

You might want to produce items for several different people and lay each set out on a separate table. The groups then visit each table in turn to examine the items and build up their profiles.

Secret signs

The children will enjoy looking for clues in this activity.

Resources

None.

What to do

Put the children into pairs. Explain that they must devise a secret sign with their partner. This could be an action – such as putting their hand on their hip or touching an ear – or a word. Choose a pair to start the game. One member of the pair goes out of the room, while their partner chooses three small objects in the room, telling the other children what they are. The child outside the room is then invited back in. Their partner describes the different items in the room, using the agreed sign when they mention one of the chosen objects. The child who was sent outside should watch out/listen for this sign and collect each of the appropriate objects accordingly. The other children have to try to work out the secret sign that the pair are using to identify the chosen objects. If all three objects are collected before the children correctly guess the secret sign, the pair have outsmarted the group and win the round.

Comments

Tell the pairs to spread out and talk quietly so as not to give away their secret signs. With younger children, discuss the possible signs that they could use before they split up into pairs.

Pick up the pieces

The children must work together in this activity to achieve a shared goal.

Resources

A photocopy or printout downloaded from the online resources of page 130.

What to do

Cut up the photocopy or printout of page 130 as marked and set aside one of the clues for each event. Place the remaining clues around the room. Divide the children into six groups. Explain that various clues relating to different events have been placed around the room. Give each group one of the clues you set aside, so that they know which event they are looking for. Tell them that each group has been given a different event. On your command, the children must move around the room, looking for clues that relate to their event. If they find one, they hold on to it. If not, they leave the clue where they found it.

If some groups can't find all their clues and others have more than six, the groups must get together to try to work out what has gone wrong. After an appropriate amount of time, call the children together and let each group in turn present their clues and share what they think their event is.

Comments

You may have to explain the events to younger children before you start this activity.

Building up a picture

The children must work together in this activity to interpret a set of picture clues.

Resources

One photocopied or printed out set of the picture clues on page 131 per group, cut up into individual clues. Each set should be numbered in a different order.

What to do

Divide the children into six groups and give each group a set of picture clues. Ask each group to devise a story based on the numerical order of their clues. Allow sufficient time for the groups to develop their storylines and then call the children together. Allow each group in turn to display their picture clues in the given order and tell their story.

Comments

Discuss how the different stories were developed from the same sources.

Bearnapped!

In this activity, the children must co-operate in order to piece together information to solve a problem.

Resources

A letter from a kidnapped teddy bear for each group – an example is provided below.

What to do

Divide the children into groups and give each group a letter from a kidnapped teddy bear that gives them clues to where it is hidden. For example, the following letter describes a school hall:

> Dear Children
>
> I have been bearnapped! I was bundled into a bag and now I can't see where I am. However, I did manage to write this note and drop it out of the bag. I hope someone finds it. I think I'm in a large room, as it takes quite a long time for my bearnappers to come in one door and walk out of the other. I can hear their footsteps, so there's no carpet on the floor. I think there are high windows, as I can hear birdsong above me. I can hear a clock ticking.
>
> Please come and rescue me!
>
> Edward Bear

The children must work in their groups to deduce the location of their bear and then go with an adult to rescue it.

Comments

You might like to extend this activity by asking each group to find a different place to hide their bear and write a letter for another group to interpret. Depending on the ages and abilities of the children, you could make the clues more cryptic or use line drawings to simplify the task.

Finders keepers

The children must work together in this activity to devise clues to the whereabouts of a hidden object.

Resources

A small object to hide.

What to do

Ask one child to leave the room while another child hides the object somewhere in the room. When the child who left the room returns, the group must help them to find the object by using the 'cold/warmer/hot/scorching' vocabulary of Hunt the Thimble.

Divide the children into groups. Explain that each group will devise their own set of verbal clues for the game. However, they are not allowed to explain how these work to the child trying to find the object. This child must work out the logic behind the clues. Model how to do this, showing that the clues must be comparative in order to guide the child closer to the hidden object. For example:

- 'Seeds/seedlings/raw vegetables/cooked vegetables.'
- 'Mound/hillock/hill/mountain.'
- 'Flea/mouse/elephant/whale.'
- 'Mars/Earth/Venus/Mercury'.

Give each group a turn at hiding the object and guiding a child to it using their clues.

Comments

Check each group's clues beforehand to ensure that they are workable.

Sneezy subjects

The children will enjoy working out the categories in this amusing activity.

Resources

None.

What to do

Tell the children that you are going to read them a short passage that includes some things with a common theme that you are allergic to. Ask them whether they can work out what you are allergic to. Use the following text and sneeze where appropriate:

> *We have delicious food in our restaurant. You might like to start with olives, garlic and chilli prawns* [sneeze], *vegetable samosa or goat's cheese tart. You could follow this with roast chicken, butternut squash lasagne, lamb kofta, crab salad* [sneeze] *or duck in orange sauce. There are side dishes of vegetables, potatoes or deep-fried octopus rings* [sneeze]. *To finish, you might enjoy apple pie with cream, chocolate pudding with custard or ice cream. If you don't have a sweet tooth, you can end the meal with cheese and biscuits.*

According to this script, you are allergic to seafood. Can any of the children work this out?

Divide the children into mixed-ability groups and ask each group to prepare their own short passage that includes something they are allergic to. They can choose any category they wish. Each group reads out their passage in turn, including the sneezes. The other groups must try to guess the allergy in each case.

Comments

Older children could try more subtle allergies, such as anything beginning with 'P'.

Further activities

Story clues

Divide the children into groups and give each group the title of two well-known stories. Each group must work out a set of four clues that will help the other groups to identify the story in question. The clues should gradually become easier – for example, the following clues might be used for *Cinderella*:

- Someone is working hard.
- A pumpkin comes in handy.
- Midnight is an important time.
- A glass slipper is involved.

Share out the sets of clues between the groups and give them time to try to interpret the clues. If a group works out a story from the first clue, they get four points; if they guess it on the second clue, they get three points and so on.

Expressions

There are plenty of facial expression sets that you can buy online. If you make your own, try to include faces showing happiness, sadness, anger, surprise, fear, boredom and excitement. Put the cards in a container. Create a set of drawings of objects such as a box, a teddy bear, a dog, a sandwich, a car, a child and an open door. Put these cards in a second container. Each child or group takes a card from each container. They must make up a short story using their two cards, which they then share with the other children.

3 Expending Energy Together

This section includes action-packed games that require children to work together. Some of the activities combine teamwork with a competitive element, encouraging children to help each other to achieve a shared goal. In other games, the fast-and-furious pace creates an exciting atmosphere and promotes positive group dynamics.

Treasure trove

The children will enjoy this race against time.

Resources

A box of plastic coins; sheets of newspaper; sticky tape; and a large spotted dice.

What to do

Wrap the box of coins in layers of newspaper, as you would for a game of Pass the Parcel. Ask the children to form a large circle and place the parcel in the centre of it. Give the dice to a child to start the game. They roll the dice. If they roll a six, they run into the centre of the circle and begin to unwrap the parcel, one sheet of newspaper at a time. At the same time, the dice continues in a clockwise direction around the circle. The next child to roll a six swaps places with the child in the centre and continues to unwrap the parcel. If a two is rolled, everyone in the circle counts down from ten to zero. At the end of the countdown, the child in the centre must return to their place in the circle and the game continues. If a four is rolled, the child who rolled the dice must run around the outside of the circle. When they return to their space, they shout, 'Stop!' The child in the centre must return to their place in the circle and the game continues. If an odd number is rolled, the dice passes to the next child. The game ends once the parcel has been unwrapped.

Comments

If you play this game on a special occasion, put a bag of snacks in the middle of the parcel, which the winner can share with the group.

Get weaving

This race against time encourages teams to make maximum effort.

Resources

None. You need plenty of space to move around in.

What to do

Divide the children into two or three evenly matched teams. Each team stands in a large circle. Ensure that there is sufficient space between each player for a child to move around them.

On your command, the player in each circle nominated to start weaves in and out of their teammates in a clockwise direction. When they return to their space, the player on their left sets off round the circle and so on. The first team to sit down having had all members complete their circuit is the winner.

Comments

Vary this game by adding new challenges – for example, each child must complete their circuit with a beanbag on their head or a balloon between their legs.

Heads or tails?

Teamwork is required to help group members get to safety in this game.

Resources

A selection of soft balls, two PE markers and a coin. You need plenty of space to move around in.

What to do

Divide the class into two evenly matched teams, naming one team 'Heads' and the other 'Tails'. Give each team an equal number of soft balls. The two teams stand at opposite ends of the room. Place the PE markers in the middle of the room about a metre apart. Each team chooses one of their members to stand by the marker nearest to their team. Toss the coin and call heads or tails accordingly. The child in the centre from that team must try to run back to their team. The child in the centre from the other team must pursue them. The team whose name was called must try to distract the pursuing child by throwing their soft balls at them. If the child reaches home without being touched by the pursuing child, their team scores a point. If the pursuing child touches the child before they reach home, their team scores a point. The game continues in this way until all the children have had a turn in the centre. The winning team is the one with the most points.

Comments

You could add to the fun of this game by making the players in the centre move in a certain way – such as hopping, jumping, crawling or heel-to-toe steps.

Group tug of war

The children have to work together in this activity to try to beat the competition.

Resources

Four PE markers and a long piece of rope with the ends tied together in a reef knot to form a circle. You need plenty of space to move around in.

What to do

Divide the children into four teams of roughly equal physical strength. Have them line up according to how strong they think they are, with the strongest at the back of the line (you may need to help with this). Organise the teams around the rope circle so that each team is standing at one of the four main compass points. The first child in each team takes hold of the rope. The rest of their team must stand 5 metres behind them. Use a marker to indicate this distance in each case. On your command, the four children each try to pull the rope towards them in an attempt to reach their team. At any time, they can call for the next child in the team to take their place and go to the back of their line. Only one person from each team can hold the rope at any one time. This continues until someone wins the game by reaching their team.

Comments

If all the strongest children are pulling on the rope and a stalemate ensues, stop the game and declare it a draw.

Steppingstones

This game requires each child to support a teammate.

Resources

Two circles of thick cardboard about 15 centimetres in diameter (you could use small non-slip PE mats). You need plenty of space to move around in. Avoid playing on an area with a slippery surface.

What to do

Divide the children into four or five teams. Give each team a pair of cardboard circles or PE mats to use as steppingstones. Ask each team to line up at one end of the room. On your command, Player 2 in each team places the steppingstones in front of their team's Player 1. As Player 1 steps from the first of their steppingstones to the second, Player 2 must pick up the steppingstone from under their back foot and place it in front of them. This continues until they reach the other end of the room. Player 1 remains there, while Player 2 picks up the steppingstones and runs back to their team. Player 3 then takes the steppingstones and leads Player 2 across the room. The game continues in this way until the final player in a team has guided the child in front of them across the room. At this point, Player 1 picks up the steppingstones and runs back to the other end of the room with their team's final player. Player 1 then guides the last child in their team across the playing area. The first team to complete the crossing is the winner.

Comments

Give the children an opportunity to practise moving the steppingstones before the game so that they get an idea of the optimal distance to move them.

Pass the ball, please

The children need to work together in this game to succeed.

Resources

Two large balls. You need plenty of space to move around in.

What to do

Ask the children to form a large circle. Number them one or two alternately around the circle. Choose a child from each team at opposite points of the circle and give each of them a ball. On your command, each team must try to pass their ball round the circle in a clockwise direction. Each team member must handle the ball in turn. The ball must be passed across the children from the opposing team. The first team to pass the ball around the circle and back to the team member who began the game is the winner.

Comments

Play the game again, but this time continue passing the balls round the circle to see whether one team can win by overtaking the other team's ball. You could also switch the direction in which the balls are passed around the circle.

Catch a snake

The children have to work together in this game to devise winning tactics.

Resources

Two large soft balls. You need plenty of space to move around in.

What to do

Divide the children into four teams. Ask two teams to each form a large circle. Give one child in each circle a soft ball. Each of the remaining two teams enters one of the circles, standing in a line one behind the other. Each child in the line holds the waist of the child in front of them, forming a snake. On your command, the team forming each circle must try to hit the snake's head – the child at the front of the line – on the legs with their balls. The other children in the line must try to protect their snake's head by blocking the ball with their bodies. If the ball makes contact with the snake's head, the teams swap places. You can also swap the teams around after a certain amount of time if the snake has avoided being hit.

Comments

The team members in a circle can throw or bounce the ball to one another in an attempt to catch the snake out.

Chariot racing

The children must work together in groups of three in this activity.

Resources

Skipping ropes, a stopwatch and pieces of PE equipment, such as hurdles, hula hoops, bean bags and balls. You need plenty of space to move around in.

What to do

Divide the children into groups of three. Explain that they are going to pretend that they are chariot racing. Two children in each group will be the horses, while the third will be the charioteer. Lay out an obstacle course using the PE equipment. The horses stand side by side and link arms or hold hands. The charioteer passes a skipping rope under the outside arm of each of their horses, creating reins, and holds the ends of the reins. They then lead their horses through the obstacle course while you time them with the stopwatch.

Comments

Give the groups time to practise with different combinations of horses and charioteers so that they can pick their most successful combination for the race.

The hungry bear

In this game, the children must work together to try to deprive the hungry bear of a meal.

Resources

A whiteboard and a pen. You need plenty of space to move around in.

What to do

Choose one child to be the hungry bear and divide the other children into three or four groups. Write a list of different types of food on the whiteboard, with the number of items on the list corresponding to the size of each group. Ask the bear to leave the room briefly while the children in each group decide who will be each of the different foods. Each group then forms a line at one of the four main compass points. The bear comes back in and stands in the middle of the room. They say, 'I'm so hungry I could eat ... [one of the foods from the list].' The children who chose that food must then swap places with each other. The hungry bear tries to take a vacated place before it is filled. If they succeed, the child left without a place becomes the hungry bear and the game continues. If the bear is unsuccessful, let them have another go before choosing a new bear.

Comments

Each time a bear leaves the room, the group members should swap food identities within their group so that the bear no longer knows who has chosen what.

Beanbags and blindfolds

The children must work in pairs to complete this activity successfully.

Resources

Two blindfolds, two buckets and a beanbag for each child.

What to do

Divide the children into two teams. Explain that each team member will take a turn wearing a blindfold and will be guided by the verbal instructions of a teammate. They will need to listen to the instructions so that they can walk to their bucket at the opposite end of the room and drop their beanbag into it. Each team will need an instructor whose role is to call directions to their blindfolded teammate. Another team member will be the adviser, whose role is to give suggestions to the instructor. All other team members must remain quiet. The winning team is the one with the most beanbags in their bucket after a given amount of time or the first one to deposit all of their beanbags in the bucket.

Comments

Play this game regularly so that each child in a team has a turn at being the blindfolded player, the instructor and the adviser.
 Discuss with the children the kinds of instructions that might be helpful.

Further activities

North to southwest

Divide the children into groups of eight. Instruct four children in each group to stand on one of the four main compass points. The other four children stand on each of the midpoints of the compass. Ensure that each child knows the name of their compass point. Give each child standing on 'North' a large bouncy ball. Call out an instruction for them to pass the ball to a teammate – for example, 'North, throw to Southeast'; 'Southeast, bounce to Northeast.'

Team skittles

Divide the children into teams. Set up a set of skittles for each team. The team members take it in turns to throw a ball at their skittles to try to knock them down. You can either have a team race to see which team can knock down all their skittles first or use a stopwatch to time how long it takes each team in turn to knock their skittles down.

Dragons, trolls, elves and fairies

Choose one child to be the caller. They stand at one end of the room, while the remaining players stand at the other. The caller shouts out different instructions to tell the players how to move around the room:

- 'Trolls': Heavy, stomping movements.
- 'Elves': On tiptoes.
- 'Fairies': Skipping.

When the caller shouts 'Dragon', all the players must run back to their end of the room. The caller tries to tag a child before they reach safety. If they manage to do so, the child who has been tagged becomes the new caller. If they don't, allow them another go before choosing a new caller.

4 Investigations

Investigations are an ideal way to encourage children to collaborate while also promoting creative thinking. The children will enjoy comparing their findings with each other and making discoveries.

Float or sink?

The children must use their skills of prediction in this activity.

Resources

A jam jar with a lid per group; golden syrup, vegetable oil and water coloured with food colouring; a selection of small objects, such as rubbers, pencil shavings, shells, beads and crayons; paper and pencils for each group.

What to do

Divide the children into groups of five or six. Give each group a jam jar and equal amounts of each liquid. Ask each group to pour each of the liquids into the jar. Tell them to put the lid on the jar firmly and shake it well. Ask the children to watch the mixture in their jar and observe any developments. Discuss the changes that are taking place at minute intervals. The liquids will separate after a few minutes. Ask the children why they think the liquids have formed into separate layers.

Ask each group to collect a selection of small objects, such as those listed above. Have them discuss what they think will happen to each object once they drop it into the mixture in their jar. They should make a list of their predictions before conducting the investigation. They can then record their findings next to these predictions. Call the groups together to compare results.

Comments

It's a good idea to collect a few small items together prior to the lesson to ensure there is a plentiful supply of objects available.

The liquids separate because of their different densities.

The balancing man

This activity helps the children to develop their investigative skills.

Resources

A photocopy or printout of page 132 on card; a length of string; a pair of scissors, Blu Tack and two pennies for each group.

What to do

Divide the children into groups of five or six. Give each group a copy of page 132, a pair of scissors, two pennies, a length of string and some Blu Tack. Ask one child in each group to cut out the figure on the card carefully. Explain that if the two coins are fixed onto the back of the figure in strategic places, it should balance upside down on a taut length of string. Give the groups about 15 minutes to try to achieve this.

Comments

If the coins are attached behind each of the figure's hands, it should balance on its nose on the string, with one arm either side of it.

If you think that the groups are struggling to find the solution, give them a hint, such as: 'The coins need to be on opposite sides of the figure, but in similar positions.'

Balloon blowing

This activity involves an enjoyable scientific investigation.

Resources

A balloon and a flexible drinking straw for each child.

What to do

Divide the children into groups of five and give each group five balloons. Ask the groups to blow up their balloons to various different sizes and knot the end of each of them. Give each child a straw and ask them to bend it at the flexible point, so that the short end is pointing upwards. Each places the long end of their straw in their mouth and attempts to keep one of the balloons in the air above the upturned end by blowing through it. Ask the groups to investigate whether the size of the balloon makes any difference to how long they can keep it aloft.

Comments

To avoid hyperventilation, tell the children to take turns in their group and to watch each other's attempts.

You could use a balloon pump and the help of colleagues to inflate the balloons before this activity to save time. Be aware of any children with asthma who may find the blowing difficult.

Taste trials

If the children do this activity properly, they will be amazed by the results.

Resources

Small cubes of raw food, such as apple, onion, pear, turnip and carrot; a blindfold, paper and pencils for each group.

What to do

Divide the children into groups of five or six. Ask each group to make a chart for their investigation. There should be a row for each child on the chart and each food should have two columns: one for the taste test with the blindfold only and one for the taste test when also deprived of sense of smell. There should be two sets of the food samples per child in each group. Each child takes a turn at wearing the blindfold and tasting each food. Appoint a scribe for each group to record any correct guesses by adding a tick in the appropriate place on their group's chart. Once all the children in a group have had a turn, ask them to repeat the experiment – but this time, they must also pinch their nostrils closed, so that they cannot smell anything. The scribe collates the results in the same manner. In theory, the second test should yield fewer positive results than the first. Tastebuds are only sensitive to bitter, sweet, salt and sour flavours; whereas the nose can identify thousands of different smells.

Comments

Ensure that the scribe in each group has a turn too.

Have some fun by trying to confuse a blindfolded child by giving them one food to taste while holding another food under their nose. Discuss what happens and why.

Strong strips

The children must work together in this activity to develop their investigative skills.

Resources

A ball of string; glue; yoghurt pots; 5-centimetre lengths of wooden dowelling; a set of classroom weights or a collection of marbles; and 2-centimetre wide strips of various paper samples – for example, tissue, cartridge, brown, newspaper, crepe paper.

What to do

Show the children the paper strips and explain that you want them to devise a way to determine the relative strengths of different types of paper. Show them the materials that they will have available to help them.

Divide the children into groups of five or six. Give them time to devise a method for testing the strength of each sample. They can use either their own method or the one shown in Figure 4.1.

Call the groups together and allow them to share the results of their investigations. Explore how effective each method is at facilitating accurate comparisons between the samples. You may need to discuss the importance of collecting accurate data for analysis.

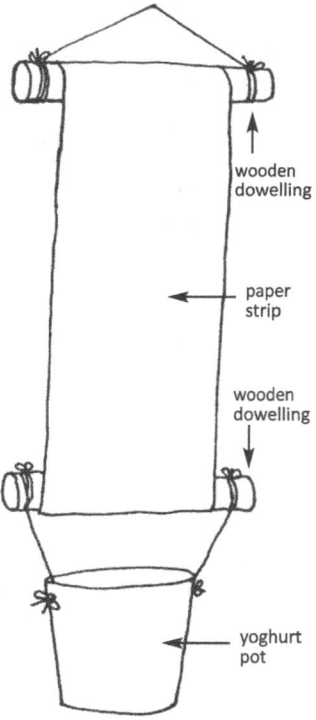

Comments

It is interesting to discuss any variations in the results and how these might be explained. You can also discuss the importance of ensuring that the children carry out a fair test, in which only one variable is tested at a time.

Metamorphosis

Children will be fascinated by this long-term project.

Resources

Butterfly caterpillars – you can order small tortoiseshell caterpillars from Worldwide Butterflies (www.wwb.co.uk). These feed on stinging nettles and are very easy to rear. The website includes guidance on how to care for them and when to purchase them. You also need paper and pencils for each group.

What to do

Discuss the lifecycle of the butterfly with the children, highlighting the changes that happen over time. Explain that they are going to rear some butterflies to release into the wild. They will also study the transformation that the caterpillars go through during this time.

Divide the children into mixed-ability groups of five or six. Ask them to record their observations as they watch the caterpillars grow and change. They might explore questions such as the following:

- How much do the caterpillars grow each day?
- Do all the caterpillars become pupae at the same time?
- How long is the pupal stage?
- How do the butterflies emerge?

The groups should meet regularly to review their investigations. Display the results using information and illustrations from their research.

When you release the butterflies, hold a special ceremony to mark the occasion.

Comments

The caterpillars usually pupate at the same time. Similarly, the butterflies often appear within a day of each other.

A warm bed

This investigation requires a combined effort to reach a conclusion.

Resources

Enough identical boxes and small glass bottles with lids for one of each per group; a thermometer per group; and a selection of materials to make nests – shredded paper, dry leaves, cotton wool, wool and feathers.

What to do

Divide the children into groups of five or six. Explain that they are going to try to identify the best nesting material for a mouse. Each group places a sealed bottle of hot water – their mouse – in a box lined with a similar amount of one of the nesting materials. They will need to take the temperature of the water at the beginning of the investigation and at 15-minute intervals for the next two hours.

Call the groups together at the end of the investigation to compare results and decide which nesting material was the best at retaining heat.

Comments

Please bear in mind that this investigation uses hot water. It's important to take the temperature as quickly as possible to avoid unnecessary heat loss. This may require the help of an adult.

It's a good idea to discuss nesting materials with the children prior to the lesson. They could suggest different materials to test. Also, ask the groups to predict which material will be the most effective insulator.

Working on eggshells

This investigation encourages children to consider healthier dietary choices.

Resources

A spool of cotton; plastic beakers; pencils; eggshell halves; and a range of drinks, including cola, squash, fruit juice, water and milk.

What to do

Explain to the children that they are going to investigate the effects of various drinks on eggshells. Eggshells are made of the same substance as the enamel that coats the teeth of humans.

Divide the children into mixed-ability groups of five or six. Give each group a selection of beakers, each containing one of the sample drinks. Have them suspend a portion of eggshell in each drink by tying one end of a piece of cotton to a pencil and threading the other end through the eggshell. The pencil can then be balanced across the top of the beaker, leaving the eggshell dangling in the liquid.

Ask the children to examine their eggshell samples after a week to see which is the softest and thus which drink has caused the greatest damage. Relate this to the potential effects that such drinks can have on our teeth.

Comments

You will need to top up the liquids during the week and refrigerate the milk sample.

Telephone trials

The children will need to work together in this activity to think of appropriate questions.

Resources

Six different lengths of thin string and a variety of containers made of thin plastic, such as different yoghurt pots – enough for 12 per group. Puncture the base of each container before the activity.

What to do

Divide the children into groups of six. Tell them that they are going to carry out an investigation into homemade telephones. Ask the groups to assemble their telephones by attaching a plastic container to either end of each length of string, inserting the string through a hole in the base and tying a knot in it. They can take turns to talk to each other using the phones.

Ask the children to discuss what questions they might investigate using their telephones, such as the following:

- Does the length of string make any difference to the effectiveness of the phone?
- Do the phones work as well outside as they do inside?
- Does the size/type of container influence the effectiveness of the phones?

Try to organise the investigation so that each group addresses a different question. Once they have completed their investigation, ask each group to present their results.

Comments

The telephones work most effectively when the strings are taut. Each group could appoint a team member to ensure that those using the phones remember this.

Building bridges

This activity requires the children to work co-operatively on different designs.

Resources

Five strips of 7-centimetre wide card, six wooden building blocks and a set of classroom weights for each group.

What to do

Divide the children into groups of five or six. Tell them that they are going to investigate which of the following bridge designs supports the most weight:

- A beam bridge.
- A truss bridge.
- An arch bridge.

Each group will test the strength of each design by seeing how much weight it can support before it collapses. Have them create each of the bridge designs shown in Figure 4.2. Once the groups have completed their investigation, ask them to share their results.

Comments

You could give older children the materials and let them design their own bridges. Discuss other ways to add strength to the bridges – for example, by adding extra supports or using thicker materials.

Hold a competition to see which group can design the strongest bridge, with each group giving a demonstration at the end of the activity.

Further activities

Games workshop

Divide the children into groups and ask them to design a game based on magnetism. They might want to create one similar to the game that uses a magnet on the end of the line of a toy fishing rod to catch fish made of thin card, each with a paperclip attached to it. Alternatively, they could create toy racing cars out of card and attach a magnet to each of them. They place these with the magnet facing downwards on a racing track drawn on a large piece of card. They then use a second magnet beneath the track to move the car.

Shape tests

Create some sets of 3D cones, cubes and cylinders using card. Place three of the same shape that beneath a tray. Keep adding weights to the tray until the shapes collapse. Note the total weight they supported. Repeat this for the other shapes.

Water leak

Use a darning needle to make a series of holes around the circumference of a plastic bottle approximately 7 centimetres from its base. Fill the bottle with water and screw the lid on. Hold the bottle over a bowl and unscrew the lid slightly. The water will begin to pour out of the holes. If you tighten the lid, the flow of water will stop. After you have demonstrated this several times, ask the children why they think this happens. (When you unscrew the lid, the air that comes into the bottle pushes the water out through the holes.)

5 Letters and Words

The activities in this section are language based and help to develop children's linguistic and literacy skills in an enjoyable way. They must work together in groups to solve puzzles and come up with solutions.

Word race

The children will need to concentrate during this relay race.

Resources

A small whiteboard and pen for each team and a selection of cards, each bearing a four or five-letter word.

What to do

Divide the children into four teams. Each team stands in a line facing forwards. Give the first child in each line a whiteboard and pen. Ask the last child in each line to come to you and show each of them the same four or five-letter word. They then return to the end of their respective team's line and use one of their forefingers to write the first letter of the word on the back of the child in front of them. This process is repeated down the line until the letter reaches the child at the front of the line, who writes the letter they think they felt on their whiteboard. The child at the back of the line then sends the next letter on its way up the line. This continues until the word has been written in full on the whiteboard, at which point the child with the whiteboard holds it up. If their teammate at the back of their line gives them a thumbs-up to acknowledge that the word is correct, the child hands the whiteboard and pen to the child behind them, runs to get a new word from you and takes their place at the back of the line to start the process again. If the word is wrong, it must be sent again from the back of the line in full. The game continues until each child has had a turn using the whiteboard. The first team to finish is the winner.

Comments

While the child with the whiteboard might guess what a word will be, they are not allowed to add a letter until it has been drawn on their back.

Allow children with reading or memory difficulties to hold a card with their word written on it when it is their turn at the back of their line.

Paper chains

This activity is a useful way to develop a shared understanding of a subject.

Resources

Long strips of paper about 4 centimetres in width; glue and coloured pencils or pens.

What to do

This activity is particularly useful in personal, social, health and economic education. Explain the area that you will be exploring – for example, classroom rules, bullying or care for the environment. Divide the children into groups of four or five. Ask group members to work together to record their thoughts, slogans or other relevant information on strips of paper. After an appropriate amount of time, call the groups together and ask them to share their work. Use the glue to make the strips of paper into a long paper chain to display in the classroom.

Comments

You might like to display your paper chain in the school or use it in an assembly.

Song sorting

The children will need to collaborate to solve this puzzle.

Resources

One photocopy or printout of an unfamiliar song or poem for each group, cut up into different verses or phrases.

What to do

Divide the children into small mixed-ability groups and give each group a cut-up version of the song or poem that you are using for each. Explain that they have to work together in their groups to put the verses/phrases into what they think is the correct order. After an appropriate amount of time, call the groups together to compare results.

Comments

For younger children, you might prefer to use a nursery rhyme.

Word circle

The children learn the value of peer support through this activity.

Resources

A pen and a long thin strip of paper, attached horizontally to a wall.

What to do

Divide the children into four or five mixed-ability teams. Each team stands in a line facing the paper strip. Write a word on the paper strip and choose a team to begin the game. The first child in this team's line comes forward and writes a word on the strip that begins with the last letter of your word. They then return to the back of their line and play moves on to the next team. The game continues in this fashion. If a child cannot think of a word to write, they are allowed to ask someone from their team to swap places with them. They can do this once only. If nobody in a team can think of a word beginning with the relevant letter, or if a child has already asked someone to swap with them, their team gets a penalty point, the child returns to the back of their line and play moves on. Continue the game until the strip of paper is full. The winning team is the one with the least number of penalty points.

Comments

Children with literacy difficulties may work with a partner.

Explain to the children that it is in their team's interest to use words that end in a letter that will be difficult for the next team to use.

Initial success

This activity encourages creative thinking and imagination.

Resources

A whiteboard and pen; paper and pencils for each group.

What to do

Divide the children into small mixed-ability groups. Write a series of categories on the whiteboard. You need the same number of categories as there are members of each group. Explain that each group must work together to think of two entries for each heading. For any entry, the first word should begin with the initial letter of a group member's first name and the second word should begin with the initial letter of their surname. For example, a child named Dan Buckley could add 'deckchair' and 'bucket' to a 'Seaside' category.

Comments

The initial letter of each group member's first name and surname should be used at least once in the game.

Print sprint

The children need to develop an efficient way of working to succeed in this activity.

Resources

A selection of pages from a newspaper; scissors, paper and glue for each team.

What to do

Divide the children into mixed-ability teams and hand out the resources. Explain that you will read out a word that they have to create by cutting up and collating individual letters from their sheets of newspaper. Allow the teams a couple of minutes to decide on their strategy for this task. Tell them that the first word you give them must be made from letters taken from the headlines only. The first team to do this successfully is the winner. Ask the winning team to explain what they think contributed to their success. Allow teams to review their strategy before playing another round.

In later rounds, ask the groups to create sentences by cutting out individual words from their sheets of newspaper.

Comments

You might like to use a sentence that relates to a topical event, but make sure that it doesn't exist in any of the newspapers in that form.

Choose the newspaper pages carefully to avoid any inappropriate content.

Picture perfect

The children must utilise their speaking and listening skills in this activity.

Resources

A small whiteboard and pen for each group; a selection of interesting photographs.

What to do

Divide the children into small mixed-ability groups. Tell them that you will show them a photograph. Write down five descriptive words about the photograph, which you will reveal to them later. Each group must discuss what they think your chosen words might be.

Once they have agreed, have them write their five words on their whiteboard. After a few minutes, reveal what your chosen words are. Groups get a point for each word they have that matches one of yours.

Comments

You could invite one of the children to think up the words for a photograph.

For younger children, use a discussion-based approach for this activity.

Question collection

The children will enjoy the fast pace of this game.

Resources

Paper, pencils, scissors and a plastic container for each team. You need plenty of space to move around in.

What to do

Divide the children into four mixed-ability teams. Tell the teams that they will each write a question for another team. All questions must have the same number of words, which should be agreed before a round begins. Each team's question should relate to something about the team receiving it – for example, 'How many buttons does Sara have on her cardigan?'; or something about the place the game is being played in – for example, 'How many snakes are on the rainforest display?' Once a scribe in each team has written down their team's question, they cut it into individual words and put these into their container.

Place the containers at one end of the room. Each team stands in a line at the other end of the room facing the container holding the question written for them by the relevant opposing team. On your command, team members run in relay to collect the words from their container. The first team to compile their question and work out the correct answer is the winner.

Comments

It may be advisable to check the questions before staging the race.

Any team members who might not need to run and collect a word should be trying to decipher their team's question while the collection continues.

What's your favourite…?

The children will need to draw on their knowledge of their peers in this activity.

Resources

A whiteboard and pen; paper and pencils for each group.

What to do

Divide the children into groups of six. Write the following categories on the whiteboard: dinner, colour, wild animal, chocolate bar, item of clothing, pop star. Each group appoints a scribe. The scribe asks each team member to choose one of the categories and tell them their favourite item in that category. The scribe writes down each child's choice with their name alongside it under the relevant category heading. Once all team members have responded, a spokesperson for the group in turn tells the other groups which child in their team has chosen which category. The other groups must then draw on their knowledge of their peers to try to work out what each has chosen within their category. The scribe records their team's guesses. Once this process has been carried out for each team, the spokesperson for each group reveals their group's choices. Teams score a point for each correct guess.

Comments

Change the categories each time you play.
    Vary the activity by asking one child to choose their favourite item in each of the six categories for the other teams to guess.

Car capers

The children will enjoy the competitive element of this game.

Resources

A photocopy or printout of page 133 cut up into the relevant pieces for each group.

What to do

Divide the children into five or six mixed-ability teams. Explain that you are going to read out a cryptic clue about part of a car. If a team thinks they have deciphered the clue, they need to send a runner to request the picture(s) of the relevant car part from you. If they are correct, you give them the part(s) and tell them the next clue. If they are incorrect, they go back to their group to discuss the clue again. Use the following clues:

- These aren't on a bus, but they still go round and round *[wheels]*.
- You wear something with the same name on your head, but this one covers the fuel pipe *[cap]*.
- A Victorian lady might have worn something with the same name on her head, but this one covers the engine *[bonnet]*.
- You wear something with the same name on your foot, but you can put your shopping in this one *[boot]*.
- You often go into the front of a house through this *[door]*.
- This part has the same name as something that is on top of a house *[roof]*.

The first group to complete their picture of the car is the winner.

Comments

Modify the clues depending on the ages and abilities of the group you are working with.

Further activities

Racing hangman

Divide the class into two mixed-ability teams. Choose a category and ask each team to write down as many words as they can think of in that category. Allow a fixed amount of time for this. Ask each team in turn to choose one of their words for a game of Hangman with the opposing team. One child from each team tries to work out the opposing team's word before the hangman picture is complete. If they succeed, their team gets a point. They return to their team and another team member tackles the next word. If they are unsuccessful, they return to their team and the next team member tackles a new word. The team with the most points after a set time is the winner.

Knock-out quiz

The children work in pairs for this activity. Give each pair three cards, marked A, B and C. Tell the children a word they are unlikely to know and give them three definitions: A, B and C. Ask each pair to decide which is the correct definition and hold up the relevant card from their set. If they are right, they go through to the next round. Continue in this manner until you have a winning pair.

Timed word association

Ask the children to form a circle. Start a game of word association by stating a word that the child on your left must follow with a related word. Play continues around the circle in this manner. Time how long it takes to complete a round. Play regularly and see whether you can beat your fastest time.

6 Art Projects

The activities in this section are designed to encourage children to share their creative ideas. They utilise a variety of media and styles, promoting diverse artistic experiences. Children will enjoy seeing the fruits of their labours and appreciate the benefits of working together on projects.

Hands-on printing

The children will enjoy looking at the varied results of this activity.

Resources

White paper, scissors, glue, backing paper, paintbrushes and a selection of paints for each group.

What to do

Divide the children into mixed-ability groups of five or six. Explain that they are going to create a collage using handprints. They should decide in their group what the subject of this work will be, as this will determine the colours that they need for their handprints. Discuss compositions that could lend themselves to this style of artwork, such as the following:

- **A tree with leaves:** The brown trunk is painted or drawn on the backing paper; the handprints are leaves in greens or autumn colours, or even rainbow shades.
- **A flower garden:** The handprints are petals, overlapping around a painted centre.
- **A sun with rays:** Yellow and orange handprints fanning out around a painted circle.
- **Rainbow arc:** Handprints in the colours of the rainbow, forming an arc.

Each group member paints another member's hands and helps them to make handprints on white paper. Once the handprints are dry, the groups cut them out and glue them onto some backing paper, adding details to create their finished pieces.

Comments

Hold an exhibition of the groups' work and ask the children to think of a suitable title for it, such as 'Creative Hands' or 'Hands Together'.

Quick-sketch artist

This activity requires good observational and memory skills.

Resources

Paper and pencils for each group; a picture that contains plenty of details.

What to do

Divide the children into mixed-ability groups of five or six. Explain that you are going to show them a picture. They will have one minute to study the picture before it is hidden. You will then give them ten minutes to reproduce the picture. Explain that you are not looking for the most artistic drawing, but rather the picture that includes the most accurate details from the original. After ten minutes, call the groups together and allow them to compare their work against the original.

Comments

Ask the children to find another detailed picture that they can use for this activity on a subsequent occasion.

Garden designs

The children will need to consider the needs of others during this activity.

Resources

Paper and pencils.

What to do

Divide the children into five mixed-ability groups. Explain that each group will be designing a garden for a specific age group: toddlers, children, teenagers, adults or the elderly. Give each group an age group. They should think about the needs of the people that they are designing for and design their garden accordingly. Once the children have completed this task, call the groups together and ask each one in turn to display their work and explain their design.

Comments

The children could use the Internet to research items that might be appropriate to include in their garden design.

Collective collage

The children will need to work together in this activity to interpret a theme.

Resources

Scissors; glue; backing paper; a good selection of collage materials – cloth, paper, feathers, wool, sequins, cotton wool, wood shavings and so on.

What to do

Divide the children into mixed-ability groups. Explain that each group will be making a collage based on a specific theme – for example, 'Winter', 'Under the Sea' or 'Australia'. Give the groups a reasonable amount of time to work on their collages. When they have completed the task, call the groups together and ask each in turn to display their work and explain the thinking behind it. Compare the different interpretations of the same theme.

Comments

Encourage the groups to work quietly so that their collages are as different from each other as possible.

Artistic recollections

This is an enjoyable activity to do at the end of the school year.

Resources

A whiteboard and pen; paints, paintbrushes and pencils; collage materials; glue; scissors; and backing paper.

What to do

Ask the children to brainstorm the key events that have happened during the school year. Record these on the whiteboard. Create a group for each key event. Ask each group to draw, paint or make a collage of their event. Display the completed works in chronological order as a frieze.

Comments

This activity works well with a class of children who are about to move on to another school or schools. Ask them to produce pieces that represent the highlights of their time at the school. Present the finished work in a leavers' assembly.

Landscape gardening

The children will enjoy watching artworks develop in this activity.

Resources

Coloured card; black paper; pens; collage materials, such as tissue paper, feathers and sequins; scissors; glue; paints and paintbrushes; modelling clay; cabbage leaves and broccoli florets.

What to do

Divide the children into five mixed-ability groups. Explain that each group will be producing one element of a garden composition. Give each group one of the following tasks:

- Print a background design using paint, cabbage leaves and broccoli florets.
- Create 3D flowers using card templates that slot together.
- Produce colourful birds using collage materials to hang in front of the display.
- Make butterflies from black paper, decorating their cut-out wings with tissue paper.
- Make small garden creatures from modelling clay, painting them when dry.

When all the items are finished, bring them together to create the final piece.

Comments

Add other elements to enhance your display – for example, a scarecrow made from baby clothes makes a good focal point.

The running man

The children will need to work together to execute this artwork.

Resources

A photocopy or printout of page 134; white paper, coloured backing paper, paint, a sponge and scissors for each group.

What to do

The children can work in pairs or larger groups for this activity. Ensure that each group has a different coloured paint. Ask each group to cut out the shapes from their photocopied or printed out sheet. They will use these as templates to cut out the different body parts of their running man from the sponge. They will then use the sponge shapes to print the figure of the running man onto paper. They should devise a sequence of movements for the running man, which they reproduce on paper using the sponge printing blocks. They will need to bend each sponge block into the desired shape before printing with it in order to create the right movement. Display the finished sequences.

Comments

This activity benefits from lots of practice but can yield some impressive results.

Guess who?

The children must combine their skills to achieve a shared goal in this activity.

Resources

Paper; backing paper; paint; items to use for printing – corrugated cardboard, sponge, bubble wrap, lengths of wooden dowelling, wool, feathers, drinking straws and so on.

What to do

Divide the children into mixed-ability groups of five or six. Explain that they are going to make prints depicting the faces of the children in their group. Ask the groups to decide who will make a print of whom, so that everyone is included. Discuss what materials might be used to represent each facial feature. Once they have completed the task, ask each group to present their work and invite the other children to try to match each print to the correct group member.

Comments

You might need to give the children some advice on how to achieve different effects.

Shaping up

This activity requires the children collaborate to create an eye-catching design.

Resources

White paper, backing paper, pencils, six different colours of paint and a range of 2D shapes of various sizes for each group.

What to do

Divide the children into groups of five or six. Give each group two different colours of paint and a set of one of the shapes in various sizes. Ask the children to draw around their shapes a number of times on white paper and cut them out. Explain that they can paint the shapes in either of the colours they have or any colour that they can create by mixing the two colours together. When the painted shapes have dried, the children should glue them onto the backing paper in a design of their choice. Display the finished pieces.

Comments

With older or more able children, you might want to use more complex 2D shapes.

Striking squares

The children will enjoy creating these colourful decorations.

Resources

Pieces of clear sticky-backed plastic cut into 10 x 10-centimetre squares; feathers, sequins, foil stars, paper snowflakes and glitter; scissors and string.

What to do

Divide the children into pairs or small groups. Give each group a square of sticky-backed plastic with the paper backing removed. Tell them to place the plastic sticky-side upwards on their work surface and use the decorative materials to create a design on the sticky surface. When the design is complete, they place the ends of a loop of string on the top edge of the plastic. They then take a second piece of sticky-backed plastic, peel off the backing and place it sticky-side downwards onto their design. The decorations can be hung from the ceiling using the string loops.

Comments

It's a good idea for the children to practise their design on paper before using the sticky-backed plastic.

Further activities

Monster models

Divide the children into groups of five or six and give each group the same set of everyday construction materials: cardboard tubes, corrugated card, buttons, tin foil and so on. Ask them to use their materials to create a detailed model of an imaginary monster. Ask them to write a profile for their creation. Discuss what should be included in the profile beforehand.

Class logo

Show the children some company logos and discuss their attributes. Ask the children to design a simple logo for their group. It could be based on their group's name or something that they think represents or is important to the group. Encourage them to explore different versions of the logo to help to develop their ideas. At the end of the activity, ask the children to vote for their favourite logo from those devised. Use it on the front of their exercise books or on letters that are sent home.

7 Drama Projects

The activities in this section will help children to develop their acting skills. They will need to work together to develop their ideas, rehearse them and produce a polished final product.

Stop motion

Careful planning is needed for this activity.

Resources

Paper and pencils for each group.

What to do

Divide the children into mixed-ability groups of six or more. Explain that each group will be asked to perform the various stages of a single action, such as a tennis serve, hanging a garment on a washing line or diving into a swimming pool. Each group member will need to hold a pose that is a part of the action. The groups should plan their sequence on paper before practising it. Allow about 20 minutes for this and then ask each group in turn to perform their sequence, asking the other children to suggest what they think is being depicted.

Comments

You may want to discuss possible actions with the children beforehand.

Four characters

The children will need to work together to produce a short play in this activity.

Resources

A photocopy or printout of page 135 and three containers.

What to do

Cut the photocopy or printout into pieces as marked, storing the pieces for each theme in separate containers. Divide the children into mixed-ability groups of five or six. Select the following from the relevant container for each group: four characters, one location and one object. Explain that each group will develop a short play in the location that you've given them involving the four characters and the object. The group members will need to discuss why their characters are in that location and how they will interact. Each group can swap one of their character slips with another group if that group is willing to do so. Give the children 30 minutes to prepare their play. Some group members can direct the play, rather than acting in it. After 30 minutes, ask each group in turn to perform their play to the other groups. If there are any non-acting members of the group, they can tell the audience what characters, object and location cards their group was given.

Comments

After each performance, ask the audience to discuss what they observed and share positive feedback.

Rescue team

The children will need to work together to solve a problem in this activity.

Resources

Skipping ropes, garden canes and small rubber PE mats for each group. You need plenty of space to move around in.

What to do

Divide the children into mixed-ability groups of five or six. Explain that one member of each group will be sent to the far end of the room. The children must imagine that a vast bog separates the stranded teammate from the rest of their group. Using the resources provided, the children in each group must work out how to cross the bog, rescue their stranded teammate and return across the bog – all while avoiding walking on the boggy ground. For example, they could position the PE mats strategically as steppingstones; use the garden canes to make bridges between steppingstones or to push steppingstones into new positions; and use the skipping ropes as rescue lines to pull their teammate across once they are close enough to reach them.

Comments

You might like to add a further element of difficulty by introducing a rule that group members cannot speak during the activity.

Masterful mimes

The children will need to work effectively in pairs to complete this activity.

Resources

None.

What to do

Put the children into pairs. Ask each pair to choose an activity that will make an interesting mime – for example, playing a game of tennis, rowing a boat, playing football or baking a cake. Allow the pairs ten to 15 minutes to practise their mimes. They should aim to make these as realistic as possible. Both members of the pair should perform the mime at the same time. Once the time for practising is complete, ask each pair in turn to demonstrate their mime.

Comments

Use some of the most effective mimes to discuss the techniques that the pairs in question have adopted. Allow groups further time to develop their mimes before performing them again.

Around the campfire

In this activity, the children work in pairs to develop their creative thinking.

Resources

None.

What to do

Put the children into pairs. Explain that they are going to pretend that they are on a camping holiday. Each pair should decide on an event that has happened during their holiday. Explain that they need to practise telling the story of this event, so that it sounds as exciting and realistic as possible. After an appropriate amount of time, call the children together. Explain that you are all going to pretend that you are sitting around a campfire. Ask each pair in turn to tell their story.

Comments

Join in the spirit of the activity by telling your own campfire story.

Where did that come from?

The children need to use their imaginations in this activity.

Resources

One interesting small object for each group – for example, a feather, a Christmas decoration, a shell, a necklace, a piece of animal-print material or a piece of quartz.

What to do

Divide the children into small mixed-ability groups. Give each group an object and ask them to make up a short dialogue inspired by that object. The dialogue might include the following:

- Information about where the object came from.
- A problem that the children need to solve.
- An action that they need to take.

When the children have had sufficient time to practise their dialogues, ask each group in turn to perform their work.

Comments

Encourage the children to think of interesting and extraordinary origins for their objects.

Well-versed tableaux

Each child will need to perform their role successfully to make this activity work.

Resources

A song with several verses that each contains a number of actions – for example, 'Lucy in the Sky with Diamonds' by The Beatles – with the lyrics written on a whiteboard.

What to do

Divide the children into as many groups as there are verses in your chosen song. Play the song a couple of times so that the children become familiar with it. Allocate a verse to each group. Tell the groups that they each need to make a tableau depicting the activities in their verse. Allow ten minutes for groups to discuss what pose each member will take and to practise their tableaux. Once the time has elapsed, ask the children to form a large circle with the groups organised in the same order as the song's verses. Explain that you are going to play the song again. As each group's verse is sung, they should take up their poses to make their tableau (if space is limited, they can move into the middle of the circle to do this).

Comments

If they are unfamiliar with the song, you may need to prompt each group at the beginning of their verse. A photograph of each group's tableau alongside the words of their verse makes a great display.

Idiom antics

This team game is amusing and informative.

Resources

A list of idioms written on a whiteboard.

What to do

Divide the children into two teams. Display your list of idioms, which might include the following:

- Pull your socks up.
- Shake a leg.
- Walking on eggshells.
- Keep it under your hat.
- Jump down their throat.
- Over the hill.
- In hot water.
- Shed some light on it.
- Let the cat out of the bag.
- In the doghouse.
- Just what the doctor ordered.
- Having a whale of a time.
- Making a mountain out of a molehill.

Choose a child from one of the teams to begin. They pick an idiom to perform as a charade to their team. The team has to try to work out what the idiom is in a given amount of time. They are allowed three guesses. If they work it out, they get a point and the idiom in question is crossed off the list. If either team can guess what the idiom means, they win a supplementary point. Allow the teams time to discuss the meaning before they make a suggestion. Play then moves on to the opposing team. If an idiom is not guessed, it stays on the list and play moves on.

Comments

You might like to extend this activity by asking the children to draw pictures that illustrate the idioms. Alternatively, groups could devise a short drama that includes as many of the idioms in their dialogue as possible, while still making sense.

Perfectly formed

This enjoyable game helps children to develop their acting skills.

Resources

None.

What to do

Put the children into pairs. Explain that each pair must create a mime in which they pretend to be holding a small object in their hands. The mime should include clues as to what the small object is. After a suitable amount of rehearsal time, call the children together and allow each pair in turn to perform their mime. Give the other children an opportunity to guess what the object in the mime is. You might want to allow the watching children to ask the children who performed the mime questions about their object before they make any guesses.

Comments

You may wish to discuss suitable questions to ask before making a guess.

Elf wishes

The children can give their creativity free rein in this activity.

Resources

None.

What to do

Divide the children into groups of five. The following roles will need to be allocated between the members of each group: two adults, who could be parents/carers; Child 1 and Child 2; and an elf. Outline the following scenario to the groups: an elf has appeared in one of the children's bedrooms, where the family discovers it. The elf needs assistance in order to return to its kingdom and if the family helps it, the elf will grant them three wishes. Ask the children to discuss in their roles what three wishes their group will request. Each group's elf can advise on what it thinks is a suitable wish but cannot reject any of the group's choices. Allow 20 minutes for discussion, then call the groups together. Allow each group in turn to say what their three wishes are and why they chose them.

Comments

Prior to the activity, discuss the characters with the children. Explain that when they are in role, they must try to act as they think that character would.

Further activities

Round the circle

Ask the children to stand in a large circle. Choose a location such as the seaside or a zoo. Explain that the children need to imagine that they are characters in this location. Once each child has chosen an appropriate character, ask them to think of a line of speech that their character might say in that location. When the children are ready, ask for a volunteer to begin the game. They say who they are followed by their line of speech. The action then moves clockwise round the circle. Reassure the children that it does not matter if some characters appear more than once.

My amazing new skill

Put the children into pairs. Explain that they should imagine that they have developed an amazing new skill, such as the ability to live underwater or the ability to fly. In pairs, ask the children to imagine what their new skill will enable them to do. Ask each child in turn to explain their thoughts to their partner.

Quickfire sentences

Prepare a set of cards each with a different location written on it. Put the cards into a container. Pull out a card and choose a volunteer to make up a sentence about being in the named location. It does not have to be true. Choose a different child to tackle the next location.

8 Activities for Outdoors

The activities in this section are best suited to a large open space, such as a playground. The children will have the opportunity to enjoy the freedom of being outdoors, as well as benefiting from the fresh air.

Box the balls

This active team game offers the chance for plenty of exercise.

Resources

Two cardboard boxes; three small balls or beanbags for each member of two of the four teams.

What to do

Divide the children into four mixed-ability groups. Give each child in two of the teams three balls/beanbags each. Place a cardboard box at either end of the playing area. Allocate a box to each of the teams with balls/beanbags. They have to throw their balls/beanbags into it. Each box is defended by one of the two remaining teams. Each defending team must stand a metre away from their box. The attacking team must try to find gaps in the defenders' cordon through which they can throw their balls/beanbags into the box. After five minutes, stop the game and count how many balls/beanbags are in each of the boxes. The teams swap roles and a new game begins.

Comments

You might want to hold a knock-out competition between the teams; or try a game with fewer defenders to make their job more difficult.

Add or subtract?

This exciting game also helps to develop children's mental calculation skills.

Resources

None.

What to do

Ask the children to form a circle and number the children consecutively around it. Call out two numbers followed by an instruction to 'add' or 'subtract' – for example, 'Twenty-two and six – subtract.' You might want to avoid calculations that result in negative numbers. The two children with the numbers you called leave their places in the circle and run around the outside of it in a clockwise direction. The winner is the child who enters the circle through the space they created and answers the calculation correctly. This might not be the quickest runner. The winner can call the numbers and instruction for the next round.

Comments

You could simplify this game by using a smaller range of numbers.

Activities for Outdoors 89

Armchair hockey

This activity promotes positive group dynamics.

Resources

A large soft ball or inflated balloon; four PE markers; a chair and a hockey stick for each child.

What to do

Create a goal at either end of the playing area using two of the PE markers. Arrange the chairs as shown in Figure 8.1. The white chairs indicate one team and the black chairs the other team.

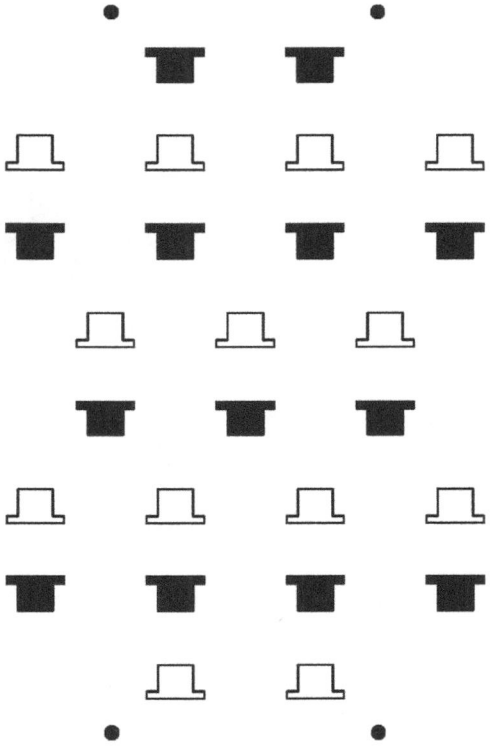

Divide the children into two mixed-ability teams. Arrange each team member so that they are sitting on an appropriate chair. Give each child a hockey stick – this could be a Unihoc stick or a rolled-up tube of newspaper. Each team must work together to try to score a point by getting the ball/balloon into their opponent's goal. Players should remain seated throughout the game.

Comments

You might need a couple of adults to retrieve the ball/balloon should it go out of play.

Colourful steps

The children will enjoy the element of chance involved in this activity.

Resources

A large dice with plastic pockets; six pieces of card, six different coloured pens and six pieces of chalk – one to match each colour of the pens.

What to do

Colour each piece of card with one of the pens. Insert each card in one of the dice's pockets. Give six children a piece of chalk each. Ask each child to draw 20 steppingstones in a line from one end of the playing area to the other. Choose a child to stand at the beginning of each line of steppingstones. Roll the dice for each child in turn. If the colour of their steppingstones is shown on the dice, they move forward one steppingstone. Ask the spectators to guess who will be the last to reach the end of their line of steppingstones.

Comments

Use fewer steppingstones for a quicker game. If you can't use chalk on your playing area, use non-slip PE markers.

Crossing countries

The children will enjoy the fast pace of this exciting activity.

Resources

A whiteboard and pen.

What to do

Write a list of ten countries on the whiteboard. Divide the children into ten groups and ask each group to choose a country from the list. Ensure that each group has chosen a different one. Tell the children to remember which country their group has chosen. Ask them to form a large circle, with each child ensuring that they are not standing next to another member of their group. Choose one child to stand in the centre of the circle. Ask them to call out the name of a country from the list, but not that of their own group. The children in the named group must attempt to swap places with each other without being tagged by the child in the centre. If the child in the centre does tag a child, the tagged child becomes the new caller. If they are unsuccessful, allow them two more opportunities to call a country and attempt to tag a child before picking a child to replace them.

Comments

You could vary the game by placing a blindfold on the caller or by requiring the children to cross the circle using heel-to-toe steps.

A spoonful of water

This energetic activity helps improve concentration and coordination.

Resources

A measuring jug, a bowl of water and a dessertspoon per team.

What to do

Divide the children into mixed-ability teams of five or six. Ask each team to line up facing the same way at one end of the playing area. Place a measuring jug opposite each team at the other end of the playing area. Give a dessertspoon to the player at the front of each team's line. Place a bowl of water by the side of each of these players. On your command, each child holding a spoon must take a spoonful of water from their bowl, cross the playing area and deposit the water into their jug. They then run back to their team and pass the spoon to the next child in their line, who repeats the process. The winning team is the one that has the most water in their jug after five minutes.

Comments

You might like to try this game as a three-legged race, with each team member having a spoon.

Passing palette

The children will need to work together to succeed in this activity.

Resources

A whiteboard and a pen; two bouncy balls.

What to do

Ask the children to stand in a circle. Discuss the different ways in which they could pass a ball round the circle. List them on the whiteboard and write a colour next to each one. Examples could include the following:

- Red: Pass the ball from hand to hand in front.
- Blue: Pass the ball from hand to hand behind their backs.
- Green: Bounce the ball from hand to hand in front.
- Yellow: All face the same direction and pass the ball between their legs.
- Black: All face the same direction and pass the ball over their heads.

Give a ball to one child and call out a colour. They pass the ball to the child on their left in the relevant manner. This continues round the circle. Call out other colours as the ball progresses. The children must react accordingly. Start the action with one ball, calling out different colours. Once the children are proficient at this, introduce a second ball travelling in the opposite direction around the circle.

Comments

See how quickly you can change the colours before the activity breaks down.

Cuckoo

The children will enjoy this fast active game.

Resources

None.

What to do

Choose a child to be the cuckoo. Put the other children into pairs. You may need to join in if one child is left without a partner. Choose one pair to be the cats. Ask the other pairs to find a space in the playing area and have one child in each pair stand behind their partner. The cats must try to catch the cuckoo. If the cuckoo stands behind the child at the back in a pair and says 'Cuckoo', the child at the front of that pair becomes the new cuckoo. Swap roles once the cats have caught the cuckoo or an agreed amount of time has elapsed.

Comments

Increase the number of cats or cuckoos to make the game more challenging.

Charitable actions

This requires the children to collaborate in groups to devise an activity.

Resources

Paper and pencils; any equipment that the children may need subsequently.

What to do

Divide the children into groups of five or six. Discuss the games that they enjoy playing during playtime. Explain that each group needs to devise a game or activity that will raise money for a chosen charity – for example, by charging people a small fee to participate or requiring spectators to pay to watch. Ask the groups to plan their game on paper beforehand. Allow time for the activities to be trialled and for feedback to be given before the event.

Comments

You might want to organise a special launch party for the games in order to maximise the amount of money that you raise for your chosen charity.

Animal magic

This active game helps to develop children's listening skills.

Resources

A PE marker.

What to do

Divide the children into groups of six. Number the members of each team from one to six. Choose a number of animals and assign a particular way of moving to each one – for example:

- Horse: Gallop.
- Bear: Walk on all fours.
- Snail: Take heel-to-toe steps.
- Kangaroo: Jump.
- Caterpillar: Crawl.
- Rabbit: Hop on all fours.

Ask the children to stand in a large circle, ensuring that they are not next to someone from their team. Place the PE marker in the centre of the circle. Call out a number and an animal. On your command, the children with that number race to the centre of the circle in the manner assigned to the animal named. The first one to touch the marker earns a point for their team.

Comments

You might want each team to number their members in decreasing order of physical ability, to ensure that each round is as competitive as possible.

Playground projects

In this activity, the children invent new games which they can play in the playground throughout the year.

Resources

Coloured chalk.

What to do

Divide the children into groups of five or six. Explain that each group will devise a playground game that includes some playground markings of their own design. Discuss the games that the children currently play that involve markings. Explain that the games they devise must:

- Have a clear goal.
- Be simple to understand.
- Be easy to play.
- Have straightforward markings.

Ask each group to consider these factors as they design their game. Give each group some chalk once all the games are finished so that they can draw their markings on the playground. Allow time for the groups to share their games with each other.

Comments

You might like to review the activity, asking the children what they found difficult about it and why, focusing on how to avoid these problems next time.

Further activities

Treasure trails

The open space and numerous hiding places of a playground make it an ideal location for creating treasure trails. Ask groups to write sets of clues leading to something that they have hidden. Give these to other children to attempt to follow.

Group cleans

Divide the children into five groups and assign each group a different day of the school week. On their group's day, the relevant children spend some time tidying the playground. If they are collecting litter, ensure that they wear disposable protective gloves. Appoint two adults in the school to award each group marks out of ten for the quality of their work. This activity might not be appropriate for all school settings.

Up and down

Divide the children into two teams and ask each team to stand in a circle. Choose one child from each team to stand in the centre of their circle holding a large soft ball. Make sure that the children you choose are good at throwing and catching. On your command, the child in the centre of each circle throws the ball to a child in their circle. Once this child has caught it, they throw it back to the child in the centre and sit down. This process continues around the circle. The child in the centre then throws the ball to each of the seated children in turn. When they each throw the ball back, they stand up. The first team to have all team members standing again is the winner.

9 Rhythm and Dance

The activities in this section focus on movement, music, rhythm and dance. The children work in groups to devise, practise and perform their work. Co-operation is an essential element of the activities.

Clap happy

This activity involves a lot of concentration.

Resources

None.

What to do

Devise five short clapping phrases before introducing this activity – for example:

- Two claps in quick succession.
- A loud clap followed by a quiet clap.
- Four claps in quick succession.
- Two quiet claps.
- Four claps with a distinct rhythm.

Divide the children into groups of five. Number the members of each group from one to five. Explain that you will teach each child a clapping phrase, which they will then need to teach to the rest of their group. Ask all the children numbered one to come forward. Teach them one of your chosen clapping phrases and ask them to go back to their respective groups and teach it to their teammates. Repeat the process with the other children in each group, teaching each one a different phrase. Once all the children have taught their phrase to their group, call the groups together and have them perform the sequence in order.

Comments

Ensure that the groups leave a pause between each phrase of the sequence so that these phrases remain distinct.

While the groups are practising, perform the sequence to one side for their reference.

Taking steps

Children work in groups on a dance sequence in this activity.

Resources

None.

What to do

Divide the children into groups of six and allocate each group an event in the life of a family who live in remote area. For example, these events might include:

- Celebrating a birth.
- Foraging for food.
- Celebrating a harvest.
- Defending their land from wild animals.
- Mourning a death.

You might want to ask the children for suggestions.

Ask each group to devise a short dance sequence that depicts their event. Their movements should reflect the activity and mood of the specific event. Give the groups sufficient time to practise their sequence before asking each in turn to perform their work. Encourage those watching to provide constructive feedback.

Comments

You might like to extend the activity by asking groups to set their work to appropriate music chosen by you or the children.

Stepping out

This cooperative activity promotes focus and coordination.

Resources

None.

What to do

Ask the children to form a circle. Explain that they are each going to contribute two dance steps to a long sequence. Choose a child to begin. They perform two simple steps, such as tapping their right heel on the ground followed by pointing their right toes forward. The child on their left repeats these steps and adds a further two. This pattern continues around the circle, with each child performing the steps of those before them and then adding their own contribution. If someone is struggling to remember parts of the sequence, they can ask others for help. If the sequence is passed around the whole circle without any prompting being required, allow the whole class to perform it in unison.

Comments

Reassure the group that it is acceptable to repeat steps that have already been used in the sequence.

Divide the group into smaller circles if a whole-circle sequence would be too long for your group to remember.

We're the best

In this activity, the children draw on their imaginations and rhyming skills.

Resources

A pencil and a photocopy or printout of page 136 for each group.

What to do

Divide the children into groups of four or five. Give each a photocopy or printout of page 136 and a pencil. Read the poem on the photocopy or printout together, noting the missing lines and the rhythm of the piece. Ask each group to discuss what the missing lines might be. When they have agreed on this, ask them to choose a scribe to write down their group's lines in the appropriate places on their sheet. After a suitable amount of time, call the groups together and ask each group to read their poem aloud.

Comments

Make a display of the poems, placing a printout of a digital photograph of each group next to their poem.

Standing ovation

This activity involves both concentration and teamwork.

Resources

None.

What to do

Ask the children to stand in a circle. You will need to join in too. Ask them to each hold out their right hand, palm facing upward. Use your left hand to clap the upturned palm of the child on your left. This child repeats the process with the child on their left and so on around the circle. Allow the clap to travel some way round the circle before sending a second one in the same manner. See how many claps you can have travelling around the circle at once before someone makes a mistake.

Comments

Try repeating the activity with clap sequences to make it more complex.

Symbolic sequences

The children will need to pool their creative ideas in this activity.

Resources

A whiteboard and a pen.

What to do

Write the following words on the whiteboard: 'morning', 'summer', 'winter', 'death', 'birth', 'river', 'bird' and 'storm'. Divide the children into groups of four or five. Explain that the groups will be depicting the things listed on the whiteboard symbolically through dance movements. Give the groups some time to devise suitable moves to represent each item. Ask each group to link their movements into a dance sequence. Allow some further time for this before calling the groups together and asking each to present their sequence in turn.

Comments

You could extend this activity by asking each group to set its sequence to a piece of music of their choosing.

Talking drums

This activity requires the children to work together to communicate effectively.

Resources

A whiteboard and a pen; paper, pencils and a number of small drums for each group.

What to do

Divide the children into five or six groups. Explain that each group must devise a way to send simple messages using their drums. They should use tempo, volume and rhythm to help make the meaning clear – for example, a loud drumbeat with a steady tempo might be suitable for a warning message, whereas a message of celebration might use a lighter drumbeat with a faster rhythm. Write the following messages on the whiteboard and ask each group to compose a short piece for each:

- Come to a celebration.
- We have had a good harvest.
- Our chief has died.
- Come home.
- Enemy approaching.
- Keep away.

When the children have completed their compositions, call the groups together and ask each to play their messages in turn.

Comments

Ask the children to devise a written method to record their compositions.

Back and forth

The children perform a simple dance routine in this activity.

Resources

A dance track with a clear rhythm.

What to do

Play the music and tell the children to listen to the beat. Ask each child to devise a simple dance routine of between four and eight movements. Give each child a number, starting from one. Ask the odd numbers to stand in a line in numerical order. Ask the even numbers to stand in a line in numerical order facing the odd numbers. When you play the music again, Child 1 shows their routine to Child 2, who then performs it to Child 3 and so on down the lines. When the routine reaches the final child in the even line, they perform their routine to the child opposite them and this new routine travels back up the lines. When this routine has reached the ends of the lines, Child 1 and the child at the far end of the even line go to the opposite end of their respective lines and the process begins again with Child 3.

Comments

If you find that the children are having difficulties remembering the routine after one demonstration, discuss how this might be overcome.

It's all in the name

This is a fun and creative way to help children remember each other's names.

Resources

None.

What to do

Divide the children into groups of five. Explain that they are going to think of a different way to say the first name of each member of their group. For example, they might stress the beginning of the name 'Susan' so that it sounds like the hiss of a snake. The name 'Pritpal' could be broken down into syllables, with each syllable accompanied by a clap when it is spoken. Encourage the children to try different styles and voices before making their final choices. Call the groups together and let them in turn demonstrate their work.

Comments

You might want to incorporate percussion instruments into this activity, with groups deciding which instrument best suits the way each name in their group is performed.

Fruit juice

In this activity, the children demonstrate through movement how a process might unfold.

Resources

None.

What to do

Divide the children into groups of five. Explain that they are going to think up a sequence of movements to represent the different stages involved in processing oranges to produce a carton of juice. Each child in the group must perform a specific part of the process. The process might be as follows:

- Child 1 washes the fruit.
- Child 2 cuts the fruit in half.
- Child 3 squeezes the juice out of the fruit.
- Child 4 filters the juice.
- Child 5 pours the juice into a carton and seals the carton.

Stress that group members should work together to produce a smooth sequence of actions.

Give the groups a set time to develop their sequences before calling them together. Ask each group in turn to demonstrate their sequence.

Comments

You could ask the groups to set their movements to an appropriate piece of music.

Further activities

Seasons

Divide the children into four groups and give each group the name of a season. Ask them to choose a suitable piece of recorded music that evokes their season and then create a short dance to the music that represents their season.

Plays for assembly

Divide the children into five groups. Give each group one of your school or classroom rules and ask them to write a short play that illustrates its use. When the plays are ready, arrange for each group to perform their work in an assembly. Ask the other children to identify the rule being depicted.

Team conga

Divide the children into two or three teams. Play some popular music and ask each team to practise doing the conga to it. Team members must work hard to synchronise their movements. After they have practised, ask each team in turn to perform to the music and decide which is the most coordinated.

10 Construction

Making things together is an ideal way to foster co-operation. The children need to work alongside one another, sharing ideas and tasks, resolving problems and using their skills effectively. Constructing things gives children a great sense of achievement and a shared pride in the finished work.

Brilliant board games

The children will enjoy the challenge of devising their own games in this activity.

Resources

Sheets of card, cardboard tubes, cotton reels, buttons, scissors and glue.

What to do

Discuss with the children the board games that they enjoy playing. Ask them to think about the objectives of these games and how they are played. Divide the children into mixed-ability groups. Ask each group to construct a three-dimensional board game. Explain that they will need to plan the game play and components carefully. The groups will need to ensure that they can construct their game using the materials available to them. For example, sheets of card could be used as baseboards, barriers or instruction cards; cardboard tubes could be used as tunnels, towers, slides or obstacles; cotton reels could be used as player tokens, moveable pieces or pegs to mark progress; and buttons could be used as counters, points or markers. When all the games are finished, allow each group to play the other groups' games. Encourage them to share positive feedback and points for improvement.

Comments

You might want to allow groups to discuss their ideas with each other at the planning stages, so that potential problems can be spotted and addressed at this point of the process.

Inspired instruments

The children will need to work together to fulfil a design brief in this activity.

Resources

Cardboard and plastic packaging; split peas, rice or lentils; rubber bands of varying thickness; plastic bottles; wooden dowelling; scissors, glue, paper and pencils.

What to do

Divide the children into small groups. Explain that each group will be making a musical instrument from the materials provided. They must first discuss what they plan to make within their group and draw a design. Once the group's design has been approved by you, they can move on to making their instrument. When the instruments are finished, ask each group in turn to demonstrate their work to each other.

Comments

You might like to demonstrate the instruments in an assembly or use them to play along with a suitable piece of recorded music.

Are you receiving me?

This is an enjoyable problem-solving activity.

Resources

Lengths of wooden dowelling or stiff cardboard tubes; string; scissors; paperclips; small sheets of paper and pencils.

What to do

Put the children into pairs. Ask one child in each pair to stand on one side of the room and the other to stand opposite them on the other side of the room. Place a selection of the equipment listed above on either side of the room. Ask one child in each pair to write their partner a message on a piece of paper. Explain that each pair must devise a way of sending their piece of paper across the room to their partner using some of the equipment supplied. Their partner will need to send a written reply. Explain that neither member of a pair is allowed to cross the space between them and their partner. After an appropriate amount of time, explore what methods they have devised.

Comments

One way to solve this problem is for one child to throw a long loop of string to the other. Insert a cardboard tube or piece of dowelling horizontally within the loop at each end to act as a handle. The child with a message attaches it to the string using a paperclip. The pair then feed the loop round their handles, sending the message across the void. Alternatively, the children could hold a piece of string taut between them, roll up the paper into a cylinder and then slide it along the string.

Architectural adventures

The children will need to discuss the design requirements of this activity.

Resources

Lego or similar construction materials; paper and pencils.

What to do

Divide the children into small groups. Explain that each group is going to design a shopping centre or leisure complex using the construction materials supplied. Before beginning to build their structure, they must work as a group to draw up a labelled plan of their design, thinking very carefully about what should be included. Once they have finished, ask each group in turn to share their work with the other children, explaining what influenced their design. Then ask the groups to make their designs using the construction materials available.

Comments

If the available construction materials are limited, stagger the construction of the models over a number of days.

Stage setting

This activity combines artistic flair with practical considerations.

Resources

A selection of card and scrap materials; scissors and glue; a large cardboard box for each group.

What to do

Divide the children into small groups. Explain that each group is going to design and construct models of two stage sets for a play. Each set should include a backdrop and freestanding items. The genre of the play is science fiction. One of the scenes takes place in a spacecraft and the other is on a distant planet from Earth. The children must imagine that the models of their sets will be reproduced at actual size, so they should think about the need to quickly change the set from one scene to another. Allow time for the groups to plan and create the backdrop and freestanding items for each scene. When the work is complete, ask each group to display their scenes in turn, using their cardboard box as a stage.

Comments

If you want to offer the children a choice of subject matter, give them further options or let them choose their own genre.

Spy wear

The children will enjoy the creativity involved in this activity.

Resources

An enlarged photocopy or printout of page 137 for each group; a range of small containers; paper, pens, glue and scissors.

What to do

Divide the children into small groups and give each group an enlarged photocopy or printout of page 137. Explain that they are going to design a spy's jacket that contains a range of top-secret gadgets. Ask them to fold their photocopied or printed out design as marked to create a jacket. The groups should discuss what gadgets they plan to create before making them from the materials available. They can add pockets to the inside and/or outside of their jacket to put the gadgets in. At the end of the activity, ask each group to display their jacket and explain their gadgets.

Comments

These jackets look fantastic when displayed for other children to view. You could include the children's written explanations of their gadgets alongside them.

Create a castle

Each child contributes to a whole-class construction in this activity.

Resources

Modroc; a large sheet of card; newspaper; cereal boxes of various sizes; cardboard tubes; paints and paintbrushes; PVA glue; scissors.

What to do

Explain that the group will be working together to build a model of a castle. Begin by sticking a large box in the centre of the large sheet of card. Involve groups of children in the following tasks:

- Draw the outline of a moat on the base round the box and paint the area blue.
- Screw up sheets of newspaper and stick them outside the moat to create the contours of the surrounding landscape.
- Cover the newspaper in Modroc, painting it green once it is dry.
- Add materials to the large box to create a model of a castle.
- Paint the castle with grey paint mixed with PVA glue.
- Add details to the castle and landscape.

Comments

Take photographs of each stage of the construction process and display these alongside the completed work.

Sculpture gardens

This mixed-medium art activity promotes original thinking.

Resources

A photocopy or printout of page 138 for each group. Thin strips of coloured paper about 2 centimetres wide; glue; straws and lolly sticks; a stapler; Plasticine; paper and pencils.

What to do

Divide the children into pairs or small groups. Explain that each group is going to make a sculpture garden. Ask them to discuss what sculptures they might make from the materials provided. The shapes on page 138 can be used to decorate the straws or lolly sticks. The paper strips can be used for quilling. Encourage the groups to plan their design on paper beforehand. When the gardens are finished, display them for others to see.

Comments

If the children find that the plans they have drawn are too difficult to execute, encourage them to discuss how they might modify them to make this easier.

A ball of Plasticine makes a good base to push straws or lolly sticks with shapes attached into.

Water works

The children will need to use their research, writing and artistic skills in this activity.

Resources

Art materials; paper and pencils; access to relevant reference materials.

What to do

Divide the children into groups of six. Explain that each group will be producing a display entitled 'Water'. Each display should include a mix of factual information, artwork and creative writing. Tell the children that each of them should produce a piece of work to include in their display. Each group should discuss the composition of their display before they start working on its different elements. Hang up the finished displays and invite interested parties to come and view them.

Comments

It may be advisable to ask each group to show you their final plan before they embark on their work, to ensure that it includes the range of elements discussed.

You might like to choose an alternative theme that fits with your current planning.

Hideaway

The children must collaborate effectively in this enjoyable activity.

Resources

Wooden poles, old curtains, cushions, clothes pegs and any other appropriate materials.

What to do

Ask each child to choose something to talk about later with their group members – for example, an artefact from the classroom, a favourite piece of work, their best joke and so on. They will need to have this prepared before starting this activity.

Divide the children into groups of six. Explain that they are going to use the materials provided to build a hideaway or den that is large enough to accommodate their whole group. Once they have built the hideaway, they can sit in it together and discuss their chosen topics with each other.

Comments

If resources are limited, the groups can take turns to do this activity.

Further activities

Group mobiles

Divide the children into groups of five or six and give each group two metal coat hangers. Ask them to design a mobile based on a theme of their choice. When they have completed their design, ask each group to tell you what materials they need. Once you have supplied these, allow each group to make their mobile.

Group photos

Use a digital camera to take headshots of each child. Divide the children into groups and ask each group to design a novel way of displaying their photographs.

Papier-mâché models

Divide the children into small groups and let each group have fun making a *papier-mâché* model of their choice, having discussed their ideas with you previously.

Printable Materials

The following pages can be photocopied or downloaded from https://resource centre.routledge.com/speechmark for printouts. Many of these resources can be reused by the children. Ideally, they should be copied/enlarged onto thin card and laminated.

SUPPORT MATERIAL

Behind the door (1)

Copyright material from Mosley and Sonnet (2026) *101 Activities to Help Children Get on Together*, Routledge

Behind the door (2)

Facing the facts

Where's the bear?

Copyright material from Mosley and Sonnet (2026) *101 Activities to Help Children Get on Together*, Routledge

Pick up the pieces

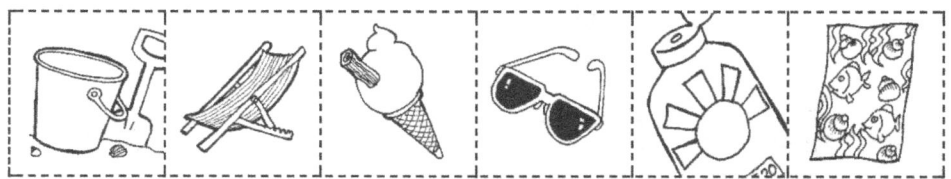

Building up a picture

The balancing man

Copyright material from Mosley and Sonnet (2026) *101 Activities to Help Children Get on Together*, Routledge

Car capers

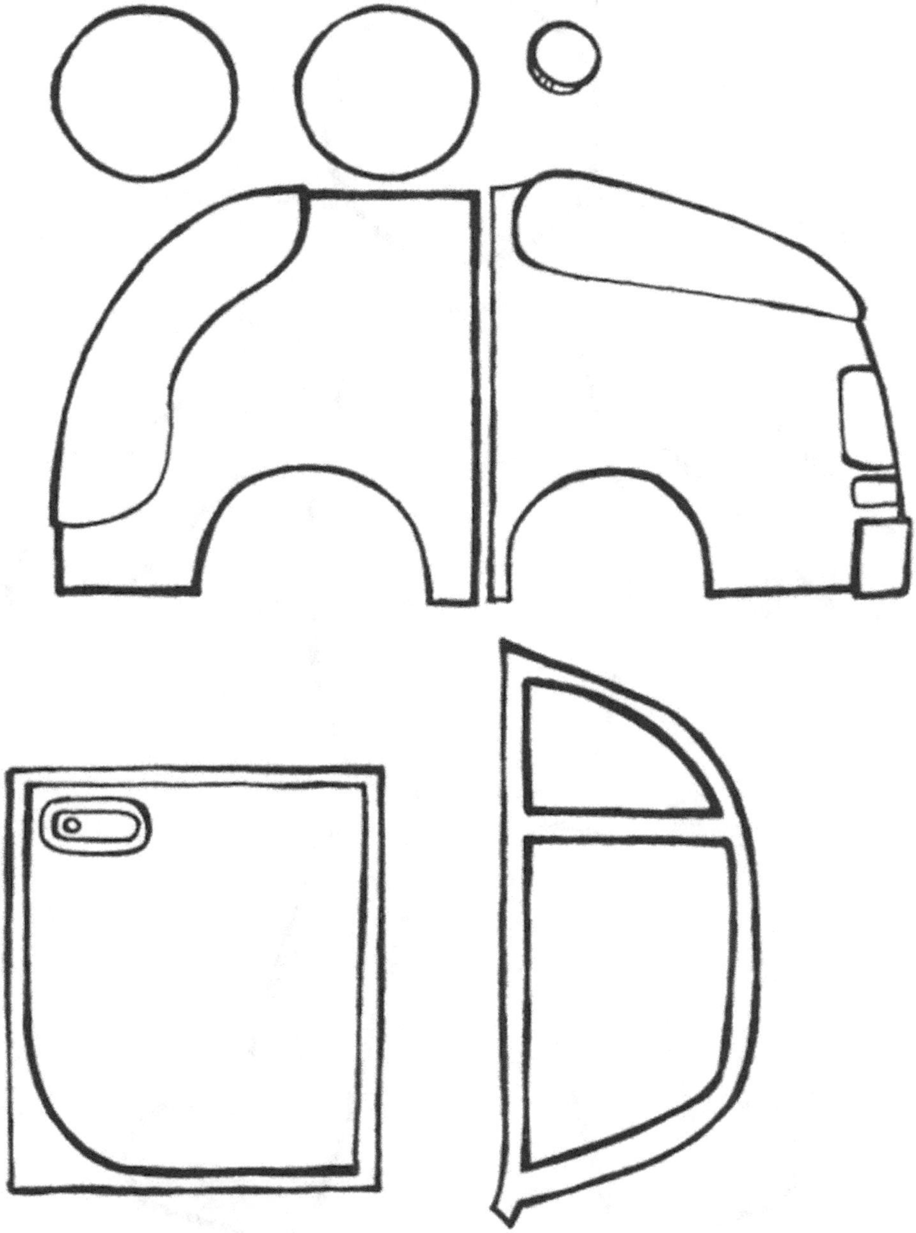

Copyright material from Mosley and Sonnet (2026) *101 Activities to Help Children Get on Together*, Routledge

The running man

Copyright material from Mosley and Sonnet (2026) *101 Activities to Help Children Get on Together*, Routledge

Four characters

Characters		
A grumpy man	A very old person	Someone in a hurry
A rich woman	A bossy person	A thief
A naughty toddler	A football fan	A superhero
A nurse	A film star	A swimmer
A fussy woman	A businessman	A writer
A taxi driver	An alien	A wizard
Someone who is blind	A spy	A farmer
Someone who is lost	A police officer	A pop star
A footballer	A teacher	An astronaut
Someone with a broken leg	Someone who is nervous	Someone who is homeless
Venues		
Stuck in a lift	A party	A hotel
A beach	A train	An art gallery
A forest	A doctor's surgery	A zoo
An empty house	A cave	A restaurant
Objects		
A mysterious box	A magic wand	A kitten
A suitcase	A fish tank	A bag of money
A diamond necklace	An antique clock	A magic potion
A cake	A glass ornament	A dragon

Copyright material from Mosley and Sonnet (2026) *101 Activities to Help Children Get on Together*, Routledge

We're the best

We're a great group. We're the best.

....

We can dance and we can sing.

....

We can build and we can make.

....

We can throw and we can run.

....

We can listen and we can think.

....

We are caring and we are good.

....

We're the best group. We are great!

Spy wear

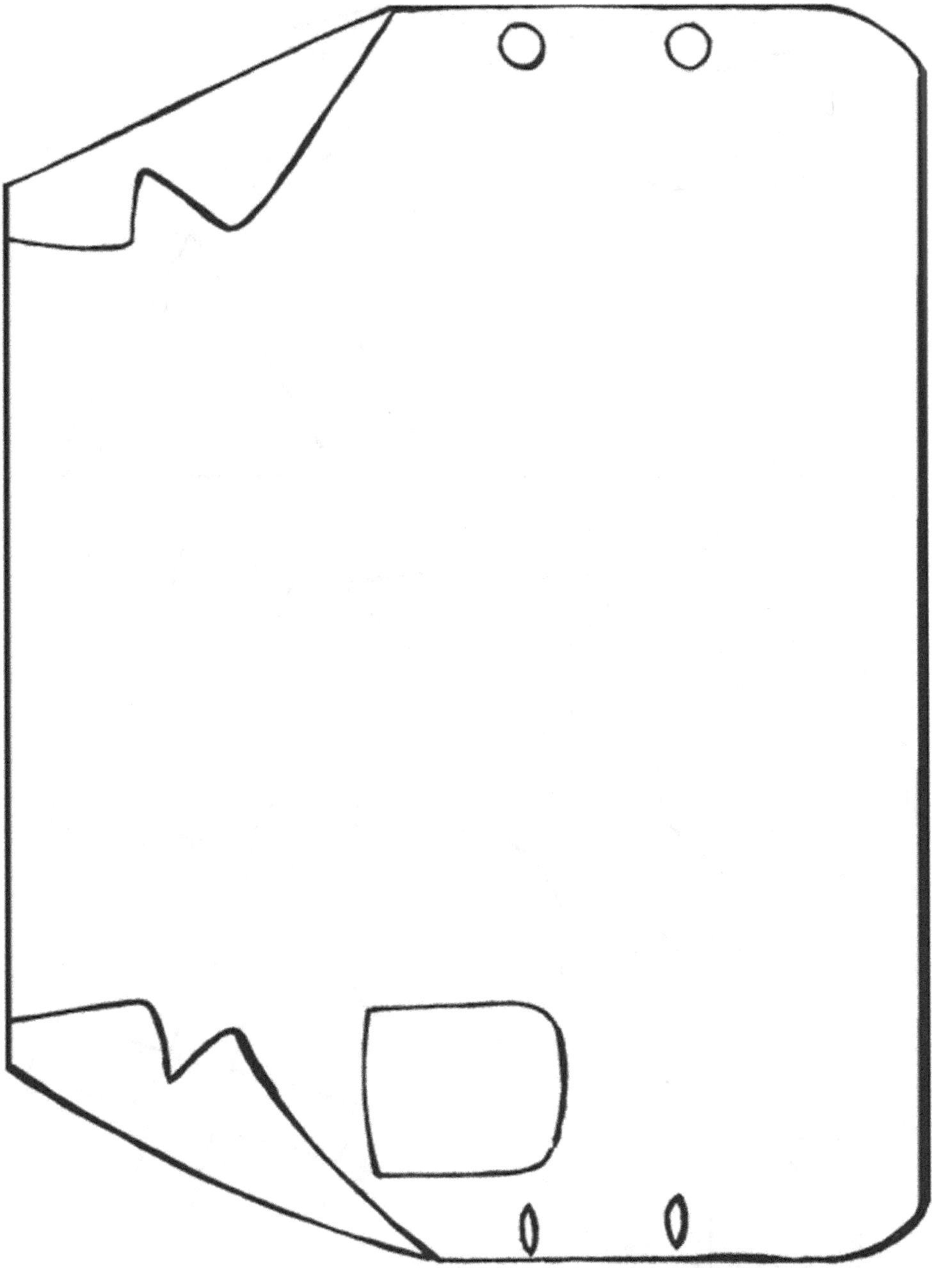

Sculpture gardens

Training and Resources
Available from Jenny Mosley Consultancies

For more information about training, contact Jenny Mosley Consultancies:
Telephone: 01225 767157
Email: circletime@jennymosley.co.uk
Website: www.circle-time.co.uk
Address: 8 Westbourne Road, Trowbridge, Wiltshire, BA14 0AJ

Jenny Mosley's Whole School Quality Circle Time Model is now well established and welcomed by thousands of schools throughout the UK.

'In my long-time experience working in this field, I have not found anything that gives schools a structure and systems to support a whole school culture for emotional wellbeing that is as good as Jenny's Golden Model.'
Ian Read, *Headteacher, Watercliffe Meadow Primary School, Sheffield, November 2024*

In our current digital times, there has been a surge of interest from teachers in how to support young people to be in the moment with others in a way that is respectful and positive.

Research proves that games, laughter and fun boost the mental health of young people.

Jenny's courses are for all educators – headteachers, teachers, learning mentors, behaviour support teams, teaching assistants, educational psychologists, administrative support teams and many others.

Books to help children get on together

Mosley, J. (1996) *Quality Circle Time in the Primary Classroom: Your Essential Guide to Enhancing Self-Esteem, Self-Discipline and Positive Relationships*

Mosley, J. (1998) *More Quality Circle Time: Evaluating your Practice and Developing Creativity Within the Whole School Quality Circle Time Model*

Mosley, J. and Sonnet, H. (2005) *Better Behaviour through Golden Time: Practical Ideas for a Calm School Ethos*

Mosley, J. and Sonnet, H. (2026) *101 Games for Self-Esteem: Building Confidence and Motivation*

Mosley, J. and Sonnet, H. (2026) *101 Games for Social Skills: Exploring Positive Relationships and Healthy Interactions*

Mosley, J. and Sonnet, H. (2026) *101 Activities to Help Children Get On Together: Building Co-operation and Belonging*

Training options to help children get on together

- **Book Jenny Mosley directly to work with your classes and teachers**

Jenny can work with your school and challenging classes to help develop ways of building class discussion, social competencies and a respectful learning community with as many staff as possible observing – followed by a debrief and end-of-day staff meeting.

Benefits: No cover or staff travel expenses and direct face-to-face training.

- **Book Jenny Mosley directly to work with your midday supervisors and teaching assistants**

Jenny can work with midday supervisors and teaching assistants. Jenny will first present a morning workshop covering many aspects of lunchtimes and playtimes; then at lunchtime, she will go into your playground and work with your children and staff to observe and assess your current initiatives. In the afternoon, she will feed back a raft of ways forward to the staff and a senior manager.

Benefits: No midday supervisor cover needed as staff work over lunchtime and the day includes a workshop, consultancy and feedback.

- **Book Jenny Mosley for a closure INSET day for all your staff and other local schools if you choose**

If you are looking for a closure INSET day to build a whole staff vision and to work with the whole team on wellbeing and building resilience and respectful relationships with staff and children, this is the right training day for you.

Benefits: The whole staff can reflect, engage and work together as a team. The day includes games and fun activities that all the adults can use with children as well.

- **Limited budget? Book Jenny's training webinar to support your midday supervisors**

If your budget is too stretched, a training webinar is available on the Jenny Mosley Consultancies website. It has downloadable booklets and a certificate that you can use for yourselves in staff meetings or can give out individually.

For Product Safety Concerns and Information please contact our EU representative GPSR@taylorandfrancis.com
Taylor & Francis Verlag GmbH, Kaufingerstraße 24, 80331 München, Germany

www.ingramcontent.com/pod-product-compliance
Lightning Source LLC
Chambersburg PA
CBHW081229170426
43191CB00036B/2326